The Friendship Book

A THOUGHT FOR EACH DAY | 2014

D.C. Thomson & Co. Ltd. 2013.   www.thinkstockphotos.com

The
Friendship
Book

75 YEARS

CONGRATULATIONS Friendship Book
A time to celebrate,
With thanks from all your readers
On this auspicious date!
So many times throughout the year
You give our hearts a lift,
With joyful hopes and caring thoughts,
Each day a precious gift.

Warm memories and dreams to share
Through poetry and prose,
You help us welcome in the day
Or see the evening close.
With photographs of lovely scenes
And beauty through the year,
Some cheerful words and wisdom, too,
For people far and near.

Three quarters of a century
And time just disappears!
The Friendship Book still touches hearts,
Stay with us through the years!
                    Iris Hesselden

January

THE great English poet Alfred, Lord Tennyson once wrote, "Hope smiles on the threshold of the year to come, whispering that it will be happier."

As we look forward, in wonder, to the beginning of a new year, I say, hope knows a thing or two and we should listen to her!

Thursday — **January 2**

IT began with an overheard snatch of conversation in the street one day. One woman was speaking to another: "It's all very well saying I should count my blessings but…" And then they were gone, out of earshot.

Well, all the way home that partial sentence stayed with Agnes so she spent an hour searching her memory and later, her bookshelves. What she came up with were these words from Lord Allton:

"If you have never been in war, imprisoned or suffered from starvation, then you are better off than five hundred million other people. If you can read, then you are better off than the two billion who are unable to do so. If you can attend a church without fear of harassment, or worse, then you are better off than three billion people in the world.

"If you have food in the fridge, clothes on your back, a roof over your head and a place to sleep, then you are richer than three-quarters of your fellow human beings. If you have money in the bank or your wallet or purse, then you are among the top eight per cent of the world's wealthy."

When it comes to counting your blessings – there is no "but".

Friday — **January 3**

" I WANT to sing like the birds sing, not worrying about who hears or what they think," said the Persian mystic and poet Rumi.

He was writing over seven hundred years ago, but I believe those words have just as much resonance today. In fact, they immediately brought to mind Sandra, one of the stalwarts of an amateur theatrical group.

"Ever since I was young," she once explained, "I'd wanted to go on the stage, but I was too afraid I might make a fool of myself. Then, one birthday, I woke up and realised that if I never took a chance, I'd never achieve anything worthwhile.

"Now I'm so glad I found the courage to audition. I've found a new group of friends, and our shows have even helped to raise money for many good causes, local and international."

Sandra's example certainly proves that Rumi had the right idea. Whatever your particular talent, don't let doubts make you give up without even trying.

Your "song" may reach heights you never expected, so try to compose your own melody today.

Saturday — **January 4**

H AVE you ever thought of writing a book? It's said that a lot of us would like to do so and some of us even manage to achieve it! But even if you are not a budding writer, there is one piece of authorship that we can all manage.

Edith Lovejoy Pierce suggested: "We will open the book. Its pages are blank. We are going to put words on them ourselves. The book is called Opportunity and its first chapter is New Year's Day."

The empty pages await during the next twelve months – now, what will you write on them?

Sunday — **January 5**

WHEN a ticket collector stopped beside Albert Einstein, the embarrassed scientist, preoccupied with his work, rummaged through his pockets and briefcase without finding his ticket. The conductor said, "We know who you are, Dr Einstein. I'm sure you have a ticket, so don't worry about it."

Just as the conductor was about to move into the next carriage, he turned round. Dr Einstein was on his hands and knees looking underneath the seat. He walked up to him and said quietly, "Dr Einstein, please don't worry about the ticket, I know who you are."

He looked up and replied, "I, too, know who I am. What I don't know is where I'm going!"

So often we live life at a frantic pace and sometimes we don't know exactly where we should be going and need someone to show us the way.

Remember when Jesus was comforting his disciples, saying that where he was now going they could not follow Him. But afterwards he said that they could follow Him.

Not understanding, Thomas asked Jesus, "Lord, we do not know where You are going; how can we know the way?"

Jesus replied, "I am the way, the truth and the life. No one comes to the Father except through Me."

(John 14: 5-6)

Monday — **January 6**

A YOUNG woman once left a note in the dressing room of another Broadway star. It read: *Margaret Anglin says Mrs Fiske is the best actress in America.* Mrs Fiske added two commas and returned it. It now read: *Margaret Anglin, says Mrs Fiske, is the best actress in America.*

It might be a story about the usefulness of punctuation, or it might be a lesson in how to return a compliment. Either way, I like it!

Tuesday — **January 7**

IN the early days of a new year some decades ago, educator and missionary Frank C. Laubach wrote these words: "To be able to look backwards and say, 'This, this has been the finest year of my life', that is glorious! But to be able to look ahead and say: 'The present year can and shall be better', that is more glorious!"

And what did he think made the previous year great and the coming year greater? God's kindness.

A year of God's kindness? If we give it and receive it, the year ahead will undoubtedly be the best one so far.

Wednesday — **January 8**

NO eloquent words of a philosopher these, but still worth passing on in a world where the command to "judge not" is as difficult to keep as it ever was:

"When you judge someone you see the mess in their life. But when you love someone you see the life in their mess."

Thursday — **January 9**

A WISH for you and those you love
To light the way ahead,
A wish for joy and hope and peace
Along the path you tread.
With memories of happy times
And places long ago,
Reminding you, you're thought about
More often than you know.
And then another extra wish
With greetings most sincere,
May love warm every day for you
Throughout the coming year.
Iris Hesselden

Friday — **January 10**

OUR friend Ruth is one of the most cheerful people we have ever met. Regardless of circumstances, it seems, she always has a positive outlook and a sunny smile to share.

One afternoon she invited the Lady of the House and some other friends to afternoon tea. As they sat in her kitchen, the Lady of the House caught sight of this quote on the wall by Henry David Thoreau and knew at once that it reflected her optimistic attitude to life:

Always maintain a kind of summer even in the middle of winter.

Saturday — **January 11**

DOES your head rule your heart, or does your heart rule your head?

It's one of the important questions when it comes to deciding what kind of person you are and what kind of life you lead.

But does it have to be strictly one or the other? Why not find the good in each and put them both to use? That's exactly what's recommended in these lines of advice:

When dealing with yourself, always use your head.
When dealing with others, always use your heart.

Sunday — **January 12**

IT can happen to any of us. One moment life is calm and sunny – the next moment clouds seem to loom so large that there appears no hope of ever seeing blue skies beyond them.

If you happen to be going through a worrying time, I hope these words from Psalms 27-1 will bring you solace today: "The Lord is my light and my salvation – whom shall I fear? The Lord is the stronghold of my life – of whom shall I be afraid?"

Stay brave, for we have a mighty protector on our side.

COLD SNAP

Monday — **January 13**

IT was a damp and rather dismal January day without the least glimmer of sunshine. The Lady of the House and I decided it was unlikely to improve but as we needed to buy groceries, we set off to walk to the local shops.

As we left the main road we turned a corner and suddenly caught sight of a bed of snowdrops. They were clustered in a sheltered position beneath a tree and looked so attractive on that bleak day.

We were about to continue on our way when, suddenly, a squirrel appeared out of the bushes. In fact, it was so close to us that it almost scampered over our feet!

Sensing our presence, it paused and we stood rooted to the spot, then away it rushed at great speed. It reached the safety of a tree, climbed it swiftly and was soon out of sight.

In spite of the rain, that winter's day didn't seem so grey and depressing after our unexpected interlude – the brighter, longer days of spring and new beginnings surely weren't so far away after all.

Tuesday — **January 14**

STACEY told me about watching "Willy Wonka" with her young sons. At various points during the film she said, "Yes, boys, there are people like Veruca Salt in the world. A little real love works wonders with them"; "No, there are no chocolate rivers but there are chocolate fountains," and "Yes, you can be poor like Charlie Bucket and still have lots of love and happiness."

Then, as she turned to go, she rounded it all off with this observation: "Everything can be a teacher when you look at life as if you're a student!"

Life is the most important course we ever take. The text books are all around – and most of them aren't books, of course. Let's study hard!

Wednesday — **January 15**

L ET me share an entry from Great-Aunt Louisa's diary with you today.

January 15th – "The garden is quilted with snow, so thickly it reminds me of these lines by Christina Rossetti: *Snow had fallen, snow on snow, snow on snow ...*

"An icy day but bright and windless. Early this morning there was a beautiful male pheasant to be seen in the garden, his jewelled coppery-bronze, green and iridescent blue feathers puffed up to keep out the cold. Later, after I had lit the fire in the sitting-room, I took great pleasure in putting down my new fireside rug, a rag rug of many colours and textures, thick and cosy underfoot.

"It was made by my friend Catherine from bits of material collected over the years, scraps which many folk would have discarded but she saw they would make something of use and beauty. I am sure that she would know exactly what the great sculptor and painter Michelangelo meant when he wrote: 'I saw an angel in the marble and I carved until I set him free.' "

At the end of this entry there is a miniature watercolour of a black cat sitting on a bright rug in front of a blazing fire.

Thursday — **January 16**

A T a coffee morning talk turned to friends and neighbours who have recently become grandmothers. They are enjoying their new role immensely and seem to have taken on a new lease of life.

Grandmothers have been likened to "angels in training," filling the homes of new arrivals with much love and happiness. Louisa May Alcott observed that every house needs a grandma in it. A grandmother, someone else has said, is "a little bit parent, a little bit teacher, and a little bit best friend."

But to me, the best description is this: "It is such a grand thing to be the mother of a mother – that's why the world calls her a grandmother."

Friday — **January 17**

IT was the end of a busy day for our friend John and he had finally to give up the tasks he had been trying so hard to complete. "I'll have to leave the rest until tomorrow," he said with obvious reluctance.

Then some words from essayist John Burroughs came to mind: "I still find each day too short for all the thoughts I want to think, all the walks I want to take, all the books I want to read, and all the friends I want to see."

But if we have done as much as we can, then we can have a good night's rest knowing that tomorrow is another day full of opportunities to continue our chosen tasks. And we will almost always tie up any loose ends sooner than expected.

Saturday — **January 18**

OUR friend Joy passed on this quote to me recently and I think it's worth sharing with you today: *If Plan A doesn't work, the alphabet has 25 more letters!*

Well said, don't you agree?

Sunday — **January 19**

THE Roman Emperor Hadrian is well known for the wall he had built across the north of England, but there's a tale that tells us a little more of the man. As he rode through a city a woman ran after him begging for help.

"I'm too busy," he told her. "Cease, then, being Emperor!" she shouted after him. Hadrian stopped, turned back and helped the woman. Being emperor of all his subjects was not more important than helping one of his subjects.

God has a universe to run, and that kind of puts the Roman Empire in the shade, but if you or I need help then He still wants to hear about it. And He will make time to answer!

"The Lord hath heard my supplication; the Lord will receive my prayer."   (Psalms 6:9)

Monday — **January 20**

WHEN asked about his art, Mikhail Baryshnikov, the world-famous ballet dancer replied, "The essence of all art is to have pleasure in giving pleasure." In other words he loved the fact that others loved what he did.

Now, ballet dancing may not be your gift, but that doesn't mean we can't each find something we are good at that will bring pleasure to others. Find out what it is and raise it to an art form!

Tuesday — **January 21**

LOVE WITH UNDERSTANDING

FRIENDSHIP, so the proverb goes,
"Is love with understanding",
A maxim that reminds us all
That love should be expanding,
Not shutting out the silly things
That threaten to divide us,
For humour, love and sympathy
Should be the rules that guide us.
So let us vow that from our friends
We won't demand perfection,
And if they'll do the same for us
Well – that is true affection!

Margaret Ingall

Wednesday — **January 22**

IT took me a moment or two to work out exactly what was meant by the following comment attributed to Henry Ford but, if you think about it, it's not that difficult:

"If you think you can, or you think you can't, either way you're right."

Short, simple – and so true!

Thursday — **January 23**

THERE'S a Gaelic proverb which translates as "I would know your gift by its graciousness." Now, aren't these words memorable? They certainly started me thinking.

If someone says to you: "Oh, that was just the kind of thing you would do," what kind of thing would they be talking about?

And, remember, the answer to that is yours to change if you don't like it – and yours to treasure if you do!

Friday — **January 24**

I ALWAYS enjoy receiving letters, and was particularly interested to read one from Arthur in Somerset. He'd been to a wassail. I was a bit puzzled at first but as he went on to explain, it's an annual celebration of his village's fruit trees.

On a cold January night in an orchard, a bonfire is built and lit, then food and mulled apple juice handed out to friends and visitors. Next, formal thanks for the fruit is given and the lowest boughs are decorated with ribbons, while traditional songs are sung by firelight in praise of the trees.

I'm always pleased to hear of such customs being upheld especially when, like this one, they remind us not to take good things for granted. Whether we attend a wassail or not, let us never forget to count our everyday blessings.

Saturday — **January 25**

MANY and various are the ways of describing optimists and pessimists. Perhaps it is revealing that the most uplifting and funniest descriptions seem to be reserved for those looking on the sunnier side.

I am thinking of these words from a philosopher, who was probably as nimble on his toes as he was with words: "A philosopher is one who doesn't think a step backwards after a step forwards is a disaster. He knows it's a cha-cha!"

Sunday — **January 26**

HAVE you ever promised to visit a friend, or run an errand, or keep in touch with someone and either forgotten or not quite managed to get round to it? If so, I'm sure you are not alone.

That's why I've chosen this quotation from the poet James Russell Lowell to share with you today: "All the beautiful thoughts in the world weigh less than a single lovely action."

This is why I'm just about to weigh in with my own "lovely action" and take that box of books to the charity shop now. Well, it's a start …

Monday — **January 27**

FRIENDS

*T*O start off as a stranger
And turn into a friend,
Is rather like a story
That has a happy end!
But this is just beginning –
A friendship bright and new,
Which is happy in the present,
And holds future promise, too!
Elizabeth Gozney

Tuesday — **January 28**

WORKING life has changed a great deal since the nineteenth century but this comment by art critic John Ruskin on what makes happiness can still raise a smile, whether we work with a tractor, a keyboard or in the home.

"To watch the corn grow or the blossom set; to draw hard breath over a ploughshare or spade; to read, to think, to love, to pray … these are the things that make men happy."

I'm happier just imagining them!

Wednesday — **January 29**

SINCE it first appeared in 1892, "The Diary Of A Nobody" has made many generations of readers laugh. Written by George and Weedon Grossmith, it is the fictitious journal of a rather absurd little man, recording the day-to-day life in his household.

The book is a comic classic, but there is a serious side to it for we should all remember that there is no such thing as a "nobody." We are all somebody, equal in importance in the eyes of God.

Thursday — **January 30**

TO A SNOWDROP

SWEET little trembling thing,
Each year you come to herald spring,
You brave the last of winter's chill,
Ahead of nodding daffodil.
Down the lane and in the wood,
Your pure white stately flowers flood.
Our hearts, I'm sure, would poorer be,
Without your magic tracery.
                              Brian Gent

Friday — **January 31**

"WHAT made you start coming to church?" I asked my friend Steven. I had known him for a long time but he had only recently joined the congregation and become an active member.

He smiled at my question. "I was walking past the doors one day when the congregation was coming out. They all looked so happy and cheerful that I had to find out why. I went along the following Sunday and now I would not miss it for the world. It has changed my life – it's wonderful!"

ON THE ROCKS

February

Saturday — **February 1**

A MAN who wrote about urban walks for a magazine once said something very interesting. From one hundred and twenty "explorations" in towns and cities he only ever had two trips that weren't worth talking about, he said.

I knew exactly what he meant – only from a different perspective! Of all the people I talk to, only a tiny proportion don't have stories worth sharing – and I'm sure if I spent more time with those few, who knows what tales they could tell?

Places and people, they are almost always worth getting to know better.

Sunday — **February 2**

R OBERT had been going through an unusually challenging time. His fiancée called off their engagement. Then his car suddenly required a number of repairs he couldn't readily afford. To crown his misfortunes, he became ill and was told by doctors his recovery could take many months.

Robert turned his gaze heavenward. He chose to look at what had happened as detours rather than stop signs and spent time in prayer, seeking strength and direction. Despite the circumstances, he began to feel closer to God. When I last spoke to him he had applied to an agency that flies missionaries in and out of remote regions, a career he'd never before considered.

Ralph Waldo Emerson, essayist and poet, said, "God enters by a private door into every individual." Is your door open today?

"Behold, I stand at the door and knock. If anyone hears my voice and opens the door, I will come in to him and dine with him, and he with me."   (Revelation 3:20)

Monday — **February 3**

A LOCAL health-food shop frequently displays advertisements in its windows, and one morning one caught our old friend Mary's eye as she passed by:

The best vitamin for making friends... B1

It's such good advice, she later told us, that she had to pass it on!

Tuesday — **February 4**

ACHIEVEMENT

WHY not set yourself a goal
And work towards its end,
Don't let others sway your thoughts
Upon yourself depend.
Think success, be positive
And be prepared to work,
Hold the vision in your mind
Just keep right on – don't shirk.
Make an effort of the will
And in yourself believe,
You'll be amazed at the results
And what you can achieve.
                    Kathleen Gillum

Wednesday — **February 5**

S OME phrases just start you thinking. Let's consider the old saying: "No man's head aches while he is comforting another."

I like the spirit of these words, but are they true? I thought back and couldn't think of a time when they weren't. I thought even further back, and still couldn't. But all that strenuous thinking started to give me a headache …

So I rushed out to find someone to comfort!

Thursday — **February 6**

MAYA Angelou wrote six autobiographical books on growing up poor and black in the American South. She has been nominated for Pulitzer prizes, the National Book Award, a Tony and an Emmy.

A hard act to follow? Well, her son Guy had some troubled times but eventually overcame them. Now he is also a writer and poet. When asked what it had been like growing up in his mother's shadow he was surprised.

"Her shadow?" Guy replied. "I thought I grew up in her light. She shone it on me all the time."

Like Maya Angelou we should strive to make our lives a beacon of light, so that those around us can always see the way ahead.

Friday — **February 7**

ROBERT Bridges was created Poet Laureate in 1913 and held that position until his death in 1930. He had been writing poetry since his student days at Oxford and had spent time touring Europe and the Far East, but returned to study medicine at St Bartholomew's Hospital in London.

He became casualty physician there and carried on in general practice until in his late thirties, when he retired from medicine and settled at Yattendon in Berkshire, taking charge of congregational singing in the parish church. He published "The Yattendon Hymnal" in which almost half of its one hundred hymns were of his own composition, including the ever-popular "All My Hope On God Is Founded."

Here was a man who healed the sick, who is still bringing music and poetry into our lives, a man who brought out his long, philosophical work "Testament Of Youth" at the age of eighty-five.

Quite a legacy, I'm sure you'll agree.

A HINT OF SPRING

Saturday — **February 8**

WOULD you like to be a record breaker? Would you like to be known as the person who can accomplish feats that no one else can?

There's nothing wrong with this ambition but not everyone can be successful. There is another way to excel, a way in which we might all achieve something special.

"It is fine doing something nobody else can do," wrote John Weyman. "It is also fine doing something anyone can do – but doing it a little finer than anyone else!"

Sunday — **February 9**

"WHEN I was little," Joan said, "I had a favourite Sunday School teacher. I was so sorry when she moved away, but before she left she wrote a card for me, quoting some words from Psalm 25:

"Show me your ways, O Lord, teach me your paths; guide me in your truth and teach me, for you are God my Saviour, and my hope is in you all day long."

She smiled. "My Sunday School days are long since over, but I still get comfort and encouragement from these words."

And so, I think, may you and I.

Monday — **February 10**

SAINTS are few and far between. I have never met one and I don't suppose I ever will. George Mackay Brown was an Orkney writer who often wrote about saints and their works.

He had a strong faith himself but when he was asked about it he would just say: "Yes, I'm a religious person but I don't claim to be a very moral one."

In other words, he was not pretending to be perfect. He was like the rest of us, simply doing his best. We are not asked to do more.

Tuesday — **February 11**

EVERYTHING changes year by year,
And some things, day by day,
Lord, give me courage, strength and hope
As time just slips away.
Sometimes I feel I'm left behind
The world seems harsh and new,
But nature shows me peace and calm
And helps me turn to you.

I can't go back, except in thought,
So I must look ahead
And see the beauty and the joy
Around the path I tread.
So on the journey of my life
Though many things seem strange,
Lord, show me your undying love
For this will never change.

Iris Hesselden

Wednesday — **February 12**

WHEN the television show "Star Trek" began in the 1960s it deliberately tried to break down cultural barriers. In a time of racial discrimination and the Cold War the bridge of the "Enterprise" had black, white, Chinese and Russian crew members, all working together to repeatedly save the universe.

The writers even incorporated this attitude into alien cultures. At a Vulcan meeting a stranger offered this greeting: "I am pleased to see that we are different. May we together become greater than the sum of us."

We have come a long way since these days and I hope we see differences as a bonus, something to be cherished. Perhaps then we can adopt that other Vulcan greeting and "Live long and prosper!"

LOCHSIDE REFLECTIONS

Thursday — **February 13**

AS a piece of street theatre, a group set up a podium in New York's Broadway. A megaphone was mounted on top and a little sign invited passers-by to "Say Something Nice." And lots of people did!

The first man simply wished everyone in the area a nice day, a woman complimented another woman's parasol, three women sang a song and a young man told his listeners that he loved them.

Given the chance people will say nice things. So how do you encourage it to happen? Should you wear a sign with "Say Nice Things" on it? Well, no, but you can wear the invitation in your expression – and you will get the same result.

Friday — **February 14**

IT was Edith Piaf who famously sang about having no regrets, and I've always been inclined to agree with that attitude. Regrets, to my mind, are only useful as things to learn from, so when I came across an interview with chef Marco Pierre White, I was interested to find that he is also of that opinion:

"I have no regrets because my mistakes have given me the knowledge that has made me the man I am today. Regrets are anchors that drag you back."

And who wants to be anchored to the past when the future gives us the chance to get things right?

Saturday — **February 15**

I WONDER if we really appreciate how much of a help a good sense of humour is to us as we make our way through life. Billy Graham observed that it "helps us to overlook the unbecoming, understand the unconventional, tolerate the unpleasant, overcome the unexpected, and outlast the unbearable."

Wise words to keep in mind.

Sunday — **February 16**

OUR friends Linda and Grant recently attended a baptism where the clergyman told the congregation that as a young lad he always had to wear his brother's hand-me-down clothes which were invariably too big for him.

And so it is with entry into the Christian faith, he said, for while we try, through support and guidance, to clothe young people for the onward journey of life through baptism, they are too young to understand the significance of the occasion and, like an item of second-hand clothing, they have to grow into it with the passage of time.

This was a simple yet effective analogy which left everyone present in no doubt as to the importance of the moment when the church welcomes little ones. In the words of Jesus:

"Whoever welcomes one of these little children in my name welcomes me; and whoever welcomes me does not welcome me but the one who sent me."

Monday — **February 17**

BECAUSE …

I HAVE a friend,
Life is never lonesome
Or dark, or cold,
Or lacking laughter's cheer.
For always there's a beam
Of starry light,
By which to chart and steer.
Herein lies wealth,
Though having neither grand estate, nor gold,
And owing much to thrift,
Make do and mend.
I am content – I have enough
And more.
I have a friend.

Tricia Sturgeon

Tuesday — **February 18**

HOW did a seventh-century Spanish archbishop become the patron saint of the Internet?

St Isidore was born in 560 to a noble family in Cartagena, served for thirty-six years as Archbishop of Seville, and was known for his emphasis on the importance of education. St Isidore was seen as the best candidate for twenty-first-century recognition because he produced one of the world's first databases in the form of a twenty-volume encyclopedia, the Etymologies. Let us remember him when we say this prayer before logging onto the Internet:

Almighty and eternal God, who created us in Thy image and bade us to seek after all that is good, true and beautiful … grant we beseech Thee that, through St Isidore … during our journeys through the Internet we will direct our hands and eyes only to that which is pleasing to Thee and treat with charity and patience all those souls whom we encounter.

Wednesday — **February 19**

SHANIA Twain rose from a difficult childhood in a small town in Ontario to become the top-selling female country singer of all time. She spoke out about the break-up of her marriage and how the trauma caused her to lose her ability to sing.

However, Shania refused to allow her challenges to overcome her. She teamed up with the Oprah Winfrey Network to produce a programme called "Why Not?" Her journey to heal herself and inspire others was chronicled in this inspirational weekly docu-series in which her honesty, forgiveness and desire to move on have been shared in great detail.

American author Marianne Williamson once observed: "As we let our own light shine, we unconsciously give other people permission to do the same. As we are liberated from our own fear, our presence automatically liberates others."

Thursday — **February 20**

GREAT thinkers have, for centuries, tried to define just what makes a friend. Yet no matter how deep their insights or how good they are with words, a friend always seems to be more than their definition.

Today, it is our old friend Anon. who has defined the essence of being a friend in these wise words:

"A friend is someone who sees your first tear fall, catches the second, stops the third and turns the fourth into a smile!"

Friday — **February 21**

COMMUNICATION is an important tool in bringing people together and it can take some unexpected forms. Consider this true story. When Erin's family visited friends in Finland, the adults caught up on old times, while eight-year-old Erin played with Riitta who was the same age.

She knew a few words of English but Erin knew no Finnish, yet the girls still spent the day playing games and having a wonderful time.

When her mother asked how they had managed so well when they didn't understand each other's language, Erin said, "Oh, that was easy. We understood each other's giggles!"

There are many ways of communicating other than using words.

Saturday — **February 22**

WE can't help it if the weather turns to rain, and the wind starts to shriek and howl but we can still make a difference, no matter what is happening outside. As American journalist George Elliston observed: "How beautiful a day can be when kindness touches it."

Isn't it nice to know we don't have to depend completely on the weather for our beautiful days?

THE EARTH AWAITS

Sunday — **February 23**

CALVIN Coolidge said: "It takes a great man to be a good listener."

For most of us, the art of being a good listener is difficult to master yet perfecting this skill can achieve truly remarkable results.

"God Calling", one of the most popular devotional books of all time, was written by Two Listeners. These two women, who elected to remain anonymous, struggled with illness and many other challenges – in fact, one of them decided she could not go on until they heard the Heavenly Father's voice. Together, they listened to His voice day after day, eventually passing on their inspiring insights in the pages of "God Calling".

This little book has encouraged millions of readers around the world since its publication in the mid-1930s and continues to be a bestseller.

"The Lord came and stood there, calling as at the other times, 'Samuel! Samuel!' Then Samuel said, 'Speak, for your servant is listening.' "   (Samuel 1 3:10)

Monday — **February 24**

A GROUP of children, laughing and clearly enjoying life, hurried past our old friend Mary one afternoon. They crossed the road, climbed a gate and swept through the long grass and wild flowers in the meadow.

She guessed they were heading back to town, a distance of three miles as the crow flies, wondered about their adventure and let the echo of their laughter soothe her soul. She had just driven the distance they had to walk and had travelled the easy way, yet there was no doubt they were having far more fun.

Someone once said: "Happiness is a way of travelling rather than a destination." If she didn't know the saying applied to each of us, Mary might have thought she had just met the children who inspired it.

Tuesday — **February 25**

PEOPLE spend a lot of money on beauty products to try to smooth away lines at the corners of their eyes and other facial wrinkles. But nineteenth-century French physician Guillaume Duchenne, while studying smiles, found that smiles involving the raising of the cheek muscles showed greater emotional involvement. In other words, smiles that cause crow's feet may be thought of as more sincere and more joyful.

So show the world your own Duchenne smile – and be proud of those little wrinkles!

Wednesday — **February 26**

EARLY, as dew dresses ferns and grass
and the woods awake
to a lilac sky,
I run.
Among low-limbed, lavish pines
that quilt the path
with perfumed needles;
beneath the morning call
of a meadowlark to his mate,
I run.
Past crocus and violet
that hem the earth
with brilliant stitching
and over logs across a stream,
I run –
my breath fast,
my legs strong,
my soul full.
With a joyous sun
fingering my face,
I run
and feel God's pleasure.
Rachel Wallace-Oberle

Thursday — **February 27**

THE older we become, the more time we have to reflect upon how we have lived our lives. We might have a few regrets and disappointments; we might have done things we have later regretted.

But on the positive side, consider the words of nineteenth-century Canadian poet Henry Drummond, who wrote: "You will find as you look back upon your life that the moments when you have really lived are the moments when you have done things in the spirit of love."

Friday — **February 28**

EMILY remembers a poem her mother recited to her at bedtime and I'd like to share it with you today:

If I could,
I would gather up the brightest stars
And hold them in my hand to light your way.
If I could,
I would pull down from the sky the softest, whitest clouds
To feather your sweet bed.
If I could,
I'd sail the seas for silken pearls
To string around your neck.
If I could,
I'd tell the wind to catch and bring to you
Every song that birds have ever sung.
If I could,
I'd circle earth and pick the finest flowers
To scatter on your path.
I would,
If I could,
Give you all the world,
But the best that I can give
Is all my heart.

March

Saturday — **March 1**

THE coming of spring seems to raise people's spirits. When that season is in the air we seem happier, freer with our smiles and our steps are lighter.

Well, that's how it often seems to affect humans, but the nineteenth-century nature writer Richard Jefferies took the thought a little further. "How happy the trees must be," he wrote, "to hear the song of the birds again in their branches! After the silence and leaflessness, to have the birds back once more and to feel them busy at nest-building; how glad to give them the moss and the fibres and the crutch of the boughs to build in."

Spring doesn't just make us feel better. It's a tonic for the whole world!

Sunday — **March 2**

WHAT'S your favourite hymn? A difficult question, perhaps, and I'm sure that for many of us the answer would depend on how we happen to be feeling.

One choice which always emerges as a favourite was written well over a century ago by Henry W. Baker. There's undoubtedly something especially touching about "The King Of Love My Shepherd Is", for it never fails to remind us that whatever our circumstances we are never forgotten or alone:

Perverse and foolish oft I strayed,
But yet in love He sought me,
And on His shoulder gently laid,
And home, rejoicing brought me.

Small wonder that such memorable and comforting words remain in our hearts and mind.

Monday — **March 3**

TODAY

I WILL turn my head
Neither to the right hand
Nor the left.
To the past nor
To the future days.
This minute,
This precious pearl
In times infinity
Is all I ask —
The sun sloping o'er the green hill,
The little breeze that stirs
The leaves of yesterday,
Trees awaiting the touch of spring's caress,
The shadowy path,
The twining honeysuckle
And the bramble thicket
That shelters the small, brown wren.
This is my present,
This is the bounty
You have given and this
Is my today.

Jenny Whybrow

Tuesday — **March 4**

BORN the ninth of ten children in 1824 Lucy Larcom knew how tough life could be. From the age of eleven she worked in cotton mills to help support her family. Hers might easily have been a life of poverty and drudgery, but instead while she was working, she wrote poetry, songs and uplifting stories and eventually she became a woman of some renown.

So she knew what she was talking about when she wrote: "If the world seems cold to you, kindle fires to warm it."

Wednesday — **March 5**

I WAS discussing happiness with our old friend Mary one day. "Have you ever noticed," she asked, "that the really happy people aren't concerned with being happy people? They are much more concerned with being good neighbours, reliable relatives and helpful friends."

So how does happiness find its way into their busy lives?

"Oh," Mary said with a certain twinkle in her eye, "I reckon it slips in the back door as they're walking out the front door to help someone."

Thursday — **March 6**

"I DO wish I'd done the garden tidying up last month, when it was sunny," I grumbled to the Lady of the House one day. "It's so cold today that I might even put it off for a few more weeks. It's bound to be nicer then after the clocks have changed."

She laughed. "Oh, Francis, you've just provided the perfect small example of an Eskimo proverb. Have you heard this? *Yesterday is ashes, Tomorrow is green wood; only today does the fire burn brightly.*"

Well, after that gentle reminder that the best of all times is here and now, how could I prevaricate any longer? And I have to admit that, once I did decide to go outside, I found a great deal of satisfaction in my day.

And even more so when sitting by the fire that evening, which was burning very brightly indeed!

Friday — **March 7**

TALKING of life and laughter, Marilyn vos Savant said, "At first, I only laughed at myself. Then I noticed that life itself is amusing. I've been in a generally good mood ever since."

I'll take that advice – with a smile! And perhaps you would like to do so, too.

Saturday — **March 8**

A KEEN gardener, the writer Beverley Nichols believed that no matter where we are, we can be in our own garden. Just close your eyes, he said, and you can be walking down your garden pathway, enjoying the scent of the flowers.

This is surely true of every place where we have been happy and at peace with the world. The power of memory can carry us back there in a twinkling. Long after other recollections have faded, we can treasure the golden ones and keep them fresh.

Sunday — **March 9**

IT'S a lovely habit of folk in the north-east of England to refer to family members as "our dad," "our mam," "our kid," and so on. The word "our" seems to suggest much more inclusiveness than the ordinary "my." It expands that concept, giving a greater sense of family.

Jesus would certainly have understood their attitude and that sense of belonging to something bigger. After all, when he taught the disciples to pray, didn't he start off with, "Our Father"?

"This, then, is how you should pray: 'Our Father in heaven, hallowed be your name'." (Matthew 6:9)

Monday — **March 10**

IN an effort to find out how stressed today's world is, researchers measured the speed of pedestrians in city centres around the world. Over a twenty year period they calculated that we now walk ten per cent faster and so must be ten per cent more stressed than we were.

Well, if ever you needed an excuse to go for a long, leisurely stroll – there it is. You can tell the people who think you ought to be working that you are doing just that; you're working to make the world a less stressful place!

CROCUS CARPET

Tuesday — **March 11**

THE Lady of the House received a pretty card recently which quoted this delightful verse:

May the sun bring you new energies by day,
May the moon softly restore you by night,
May the rain wash away any worries you may have,
May gentle breezes restore your soul,
And may tomorrow always find you feeling better than the day before.

Perhaps when you have a little time to spare you might like to set aside a few minutes to write a note to a friend you haven't been in touch with for a while. And if you can include a favourite verse to lift their spirits, so much the better.

Wednesday — **March 12**

THE CLIMBER

I SAW a famous climber,
He was speaking on TV,
He talked of peaks he'd conquered,
And the sights he'd got to see,
And just for one brief moment
How I wished that it was me,
For what had I accomplished?
I was boring as could be!

Then suddenly I realised
It was foolish to feel shame,
For all of us climb mountains,
Though they may not bear that name.
We each of us face challenge
And no life's dull or tame,
Take pride in your achievements
For we all deserve acclaim!

Margaret Ingall

Thursday — **March 13**

CAROL is a linguistic anthropologist and studies the development of languages through the ages and across cultures. If anyone knows the secret of good communication, I thought, it would be her.

So was it an ear for intonation, a study of posture, perhaps, or a deeper understanding of the meaning of the words?

"Actually," she said, "it's something my grandmother taught me before I could even speak English properly. It's the belief that every human being has something worth saying – just like you believed I did."

Friday — **March 14**

HAVING a lark or larking about are two ways of describing innocent, exuberant fun and of course there can be a mischievous aspect to such fun as well.

But did you know a group of larks (birds) is called an exaltation? And exaltation is a state of extreme joy associated with praising and glorifying.

Now isn't that the best way to have fun; celebrating our blessings and sending our thanks heavenwards, or – dare I say it? – up with the lark!

Saturday — **March 15**

MANY times in its history the city of Vienna has been besieged or attacked. It has also been bankrupted, occupied and partitioned. But despite the armies that have passed through its gates, Vienna thrives today and was once voted the city in which the occupants enjoyed the best quality of life.

The residents have a saying which translates as: "The position, though desperate, is causing no anxiety." Vienna has been around long enough for its inhabitants to know that bad times come – and then they go. Better days are always ahead.

Sunday — **March 16**

A FRIEND, just back from travelling in Romania, told me about the Merry Cemetery. Merry isn't usually a word associated with death, but the locals have carved ornate wooden memorials and painted them with scenes depicting happy times from the deceased person's life.

For them death, with its promise of eternal life, is the happy conclusion to a good life. Now that is something worth being merry about.

"When the perishable has been clothed in the imperishable, and the mortal with immortality, then the saying that is written will come true, 'Death has been swallowed up in victory'." (Corinthians I 15:54)

Monday — **March 17**

M ANY and varied are the descriptions of the differences between optimists and pessimists, but having something of a sweet-toothed disposition I like this one. It was penned in the early 1900s by an unknown poet and philosopher:
Twixt optimist and pessimist
The difference is droll;
The optimist the doughnut sees –
The pessimist the hole.

Tuesday — **March 18**

W HILST driving from Cumbria into Lancashire, our friends Don and Hilda caught sight of a sign which brought a smile to their faces: *Lancashire. Where everyone matters.*

What an uplifting thought! Usually at the roadside we see signs such as *Please drive carefully through the village* or *Slow down, children crossing,* but this was entirely different.

Perhaps we could each set up a sign at the end of our road or lane, even if it is only in our imagination: *The place where everyone matters.*

SPRING
SMILE

Wednesday — **March 19**

" **I** KNOW a little stream which flows softly and slowly but freshens everything round about." So wrote Anne Sophie Swetchine, a nineteenth-century Russian exile in Paris.

If streams could think, then this one might have wished itself a river, or a rocky torrent; something bigger and more impressive. But look at what it accomplished simply by being itself!

Some people think they might do more if they had more, if they were more influential, if they had more time. Others just do what they can, softly and slowly, and in the process they freshen everything around them – just like Anne Sophie's stream!

Thursday — **March 20**

NOW AND THEN

*W*E all need silence, now and then,
Sometimes a little peace,
To switch off from the noisy world
And find a sweet release.
We need a rainbow, now and then,
And all our hopes renew,
The promise of a brighter day
A smoother road in view.

We all need care and kindness
To comfort heart and soul,
And with the joy of morning
Reach out to every goal.
We all need laughter, love and light
To lift our spirits high,
A little silence, now and then,
To let the world go by.
                                    Iris Hesselden

Friday — **March 21**

"DO you know how to become a butterfly?" a thoughtful young woman in the park asked our friend Pam one day. She shook her head. "You have to want to be one enough to give up being a caterpillar," came the reply.

Pam wished the woman luck in her future adventures and walked on, wondering. It's all very fine crawling along, over the same old branches and leaves, she mused, but if we were to take a chance once in a while, then we might find we could fly.

Saturday — **March 22**

CAN you name one object that's a constant companion, a source of advice and a teacher you can carry with you wherever you go? It's a book!

Dr Charles W. Eliot, a distinguished president of Harvard College, captured the ethos of the printed and bound word when he wrote: "Books are the quietest and most constant of friends; they are the most accessible and wisest of counsellors, and the most patient of teachers."

Never be without one!

Sunday — **March 23**

DEREK grimaced as he stood up. "I was digging the garden all day yesterday, and my back is still reminding me!"

Fortunately Derek is young and healthy, as his garden is new and needs a lot of work, including much digging and working in sacks of compost to enrich the soil. But as he pointed out: "If I don't prepare the ground properly now, how can I ever expect it to produce anything good?"

It's the best possible attitude, and reminds me of these words from Hebrews 11-10: "For he looked for a city which hath foundations whose builder and maker is God."

And what could be more solid and beautiful than that?

IN THE GLOAMING

Monday — **March 24**

OUR Canadian friend Rachel's naturopath doctor works with her patients to achieve both physical and spiritual wellness. She often counsels her to meditate, breathe deeply and focus on an inward tranquillity as the world whirls by.

During a recent visit as they discussed some of the challenges Rachel was facing, she shared these words by Elisabeth Kubler-Ross: "Learn to get in touch with the silence within yourself and know that everything in life has purpose. There are no mistakes, no coincidences; all events are blessings given to us to learn from."

Wisdom to treasure, indeed.

Tuesday — **March 25**

WHERE THE FERNS GROW

THERE'S a place in the woods,
Shaded and damp,
Where the ferns grow.
I found them on a cool spring day –
A congregation of fragile young folk,
Heads carefully bowed
In silent submission.
I stood among them
And felt their prayers.
Rains came,
Hard and heavy,
And wind
And a brawny sun;
And when I walked to where the ferns grow,
I found them transformed:
Strong, stately, fragrant fronds
Unable to resist
Reaching for their Maker.
Rachel Wallace-Oberle

Wednesday — **March 26**

ONE day our friend John was grumbling about the wide use of computers for nearly everything we do.

"It's a number for this and a number for that – in fact, the world seems determined to reduce us all to a number," he said. "This morning I couldn't remember my PIN number at the bank cashpoint and everything ground to a halt."

"Well, remember that there are positive numbers and negative numbers," I observed gently. "If you're going to be a number you might as well be positive!"

John took a deep breath, put a smile on his face, and said after this experience he would always make sure that in future he did not forget any of his important numbers.

Thursday — **March 27**

HERE are a few thought-provoking quotes about friendship to keep in mind today:

"Life is nothing without friendship."   Cicero

"True friendship is seen through the heart, not through the eyes."   Anon

"The language of friendship is not words but meanings."
Henry David Thoreau

Friday — **March 28**

OUR old friend Mary can always be relied on for a heart-warming or funny story, usually recalled from days gone by. When the Lady of the House commented on her allusions to the past, Mary said that she didn't, in fact, spend a lot of time looking backwards and her goal was always to be moving forwards.

"I'm never going to get so stuck in the past that I can't be excited about the future," she said. "I have plenty of old memories, but I have lots of young hopes as well!"

Saturday — **March 29**

THE author L.M. Montgomery had Anne of Green Gables say these words on a hillside above a lake after dusk with the lights of Avonlea twinkling through the trees. They have come to me on crisp mornings, stormy afternoons, in the snow, in sunshine and kicking through autumn leaves. They are as true and heart-warming in one situation as they are in the other:

"Dear old world," she murmured, "you are very lovely, and I am glad to be alive in you."

Sunday — **March 30**

WHEN the 1st century philosopher Epictetus said, "Bear in mind that you should conduct yourself in life as at a feast", he was talking about standards of behaviour, patience and consideration. Conducting yourself in public life with the manners usually reserved for formal dinners would take you far, he thought.

And who am I to argue? I'd just like to add that, looked at in the best way, life really is a feast, a daily banquet of delights and blessings. So, as well as practising all the virtues Epictetus had in mind, let's remember to thank our host.

"To the end that my glory may sing praise to thee, and not be silent. O Lord my God, I will give thanks unto thee for ever."   (Psalm 30:12)

Monday — **March 31**

IT'S a proverb, thought to be Scottish, dating back many centuries and contains much wisdom in a few words, "If every man would mend a man, then all mankind would soon be mended."

Imagine if we each helped just one person to get on the right track, and encouraged them to do the same. And they did the same. And then... Now, wouldn't that be the start of something big?

April

Tuesday — **April 1**

ON Joanne's way to work every day she drives past a grassy embankment just beyond the boundaries of the city where she lives. There is a stunning display of daffodils there every spring and she always looks for their bright, cheerful faces as a new season unfolds.

One morning she noticed an eye-catching addition to the display of blooms – new daffodils had been planted in the shape of a big, smiling face!

A green-fingered person had spent many hours working on that slope to share their love of flowers with passers-by and their thoughtful gesture brings to mind this lovely proverb: *One kind word can warm three winter months.*

Wednesday — **April 2**

ONE way of summing up people who make a difference is to say that they "go the extra mile."

"But a mile is still a long way," said our friend George. "You can understand why everyone doesn't want to go that far. What if they only had to move one degree?

"Take water," George continued. "At ninety-nine degrees Celsius it's hot, but it's still just hot water. At one hundred degrees it's boiling, it's making steam. And steam can turn turbines, drive locomotives and huge ships, all because of that one little degree."

What I think George meant was that most people are "hot water" but with even a little more effort we can really move things, make a real difference.

I might have thought of it myself – but I'm only lukewarm today!

Thursday — **April 3**

WHEN Dave Tally, a homeless man in Arizona, found a bag filled with a substantial sum of money he knew it could dramatically change his circumstances. He was unemployed and sleeping rough when he found it at a local railway station.

He decided that keeping the money was the wrong thing to do. Instead, he tracked down the owner of the cash, a young man attending college, who had planned to use it to buy a car to replace one he'd lost in an accident.

The national media reported this remarkable story, donations started pouring in and Dave began to turn his life around. He is now working in his dream job, managing a community garden, and has created a programme which allows other homeless people to volunteer in the garden, giving them a purpose in life.

It is humbling that an honourable choice can enrich so many lives around us.

Friday — **April 4**

WHEN John Whittier was growing up in Massachusetts in the early nineteenth century, the poor health that had prevented him from earning his living as a farmer didn't stop him doing what he could to make his mark on the world. As a Quaker and a politician, he concentrated all his efforts on working to abolish slavery, despite sometimes suffering not just verbal, but actual physical attack. He also wrote these memorable words:

> *No longer forward nor behind*
> *I look in hope and fear;*
> *But grateful, take the good I find*
> *The best of now and here.*

And that's a philosophy to help us all through times both good and bad.

Saturday — **April 5**

I SMILED when I read these words written by Dr Samuel Johnson, "The feeling of friendship is like that of being comfortably filled with roast beef."

Now there's a meal we should always endeavour to prepare well, and it's one most of us would never grow tired of eating!

Sunday — **April 6**

RIVER OF PEACE

VISIT me with your peace, Lord.
Wash my hands in it.
Pour it over my head.
Overflow my heart with it.
Wet my feet in it.
Visit me, Lord,
And stay.
Stay and drench me in the river of your peace
So that every thirsty life I touch today
Is quenched.

Rachel Wallace-Oberle

Monday — **April 7**

WHATEVER it was they had been talking about that day, the Lady of the House brought it to a wise and philosophical conclusion by saying, "Well, we never know what tomorrow will bring!"

"Oh, I do," our old friend Mary replied. Now, many and varied are our friend's talents, but seeing into the future ...?

"Each night as I go to bed," she explained, "I know the coming day will be better for someone."

"How can you possibly?" the Lady of the House asked.

"Because I will wake up determined to make it that way," came the reply.

Tuesday — **April 8**

THIS traditional Table Grace is associated with St Brigid. It evokes a Christian lifestyle which is notable for its beauty, simplicity and generosity.

> *I should like a great lake of finest ale*
> *For the King of kings.*
> *I should like a table of the choicest food*
> *For the family of heaven.*
> *Let the ale be made from the fruits of faith,*
> *And the food be forgiving love.*
>
> *I should welcome the poor to my feast,*
> *For they are God's children.*
> *I should welcome the sick to my feast,*
> *For they are God's joy.*
> *Let the poor sit with Jesus at the highest place,*
> *Let the sick dance with the angels.*
>
> *God bless the poor,*
> *God bless the sick;*
> *And bless our human race.*
>
> *God bless our food,*
> *God bless our drink,*
> *All homes, O God, embrace.*

Wednesday — **April 9**

IN a tribute to the great poet Robert Browning the less well known James B. Kenyon wrote:

> *Still fares he forth from dawn-lit paths dew pearled,*
> *A singing pilgrim through a sighing world.*

At times it can seem like the world is reluctant to see how wonderful it is – hence the sighing. What it needs is a few more pilgrims like Browning, Kenyon – and us, too – to sing it some reminders on those dew-pearled mornings.

FOUNDED ON FAITH

Thursday — **April 10**

WHAT'S your idea of temptation? I imagine that, depending on your disposition, it could mean anything from sneaking an extra biscuit to an opportunity to steal the crown jewels.

Well, all right, I imagine most of us could resist that last example, but sometimes temptation comes in so subtle a form that we hardly even perceive it's there. For example, no-one really needs to be concerned about a simple everyday conversation, do they?

Well, George Sala points out something we should all keep in mind: "Not only to say the right thing in the right place, but far more difficult, to leave unsaid the wrong thing at the tempting moment."

If we all made the effort to stay silent at times, what a huge difference it would make to those around us.

Friday — **April 11**

WHEN our Canadian friend Logan graduated from high school, his family put a small congratulatory notice in the local paper. Beneath a picture of Logan in his graduation gown, they expressed their best wishes and included this thoughtful poem:

The future lies before you
Like a field of driven snow,
Be careful how you tread it
For every step will show.

Saturday — **April 12**

THIS piece of wisdom was seen on a poster in a Women's Guild meeting room in a village church:

"People with humility do not think less of themselves but think of themselves less."

A point to ponder in an age when this quality is not always so commonly found.

Sunday — **April 13**

ELRED of Rievaulx was a monk who lived in the twelfth century. No contemporary paintings of him survive so we cannot know what he looked like but he was described by one historian as "a singularly attractive figure." Was it his looks that made him so attractive or perhaps an athletic stature?

A clue might be found in these words of his: "What brings joy to the heart is not so much the friend's gifts, but the friend's love."

Perhaps having a Heavenly Friend who loved him is what makes Aelred's countenance shine down through the centuries.

"And surely I am with you always, to the very end of the age." (Matthew 28:20)

Monday — **April 14**

JUST THE TONIC!

TRY out a smile when you're down in the dumps,
And the world seems so dreary and grey,
Laugh at the clouds when the sky's in a mood
And you'll frighten the raindrops away!

Look on the bright side of life when you can,
For surely it just goes to show –
By thinking that way, you'll be finding each day
The bright side's the best side to know!
Elizabeth Gozney

Tuesday — **April 15**

ALAN'S grandmother always told him: "Faith is the envelope in which every request to our heavenly Father must be placed."

Words to live by, don't you agree?

Wednesday — **April 16**

IN the film "Cool Hand Luke" Paul Newman acquires his nickname by taking a poor hand in a game of cards and, with his attitude and style, turning it into a "cool hand."

Despite being born more than a hundred years earlier, doctor and hymn writer H.T. Leslie would probably have appreciated the character's style. He wrote: "The game of life is not so much in holding a good hand as playing a poor hand well."

So, take whatever hand life has dealt you, then play it as well as you possibly can.

Thursday — **April 17**

AS the day draws to a close our old friend Mary likes to read a short story, or perhaps listen to some favourite soothing music before going upstairs to bed. I wonder if you know these words by William Shakespeare of which I was reminded not long ago?

Those friends thou hast, and their adoption tried,
Grapple them to thy soul with hoops of steel.

Such tried and true friends, I think you will agree, are pearls without price and to be greatly treasured.

Friday — **April 18**

THIS Easter, I'd like to share these memorable words with you. Reflect on them as you celebrate the gift of fresh hope and new life.

" 'Twas Easter Sunday. The full-blossomed trees filled all the air with fragrance and with joy."
Henry Wadsworth Longfellow

"The story of Easter is the story of God's wonderful window of divine surprise."
Carl Knudsen

"On Easter Day the veil between time and eternity thins to gossamer."
Douglas Horton

Saturday — **April 19**

A RADIO station announced that a survey of almost ten thousand people found we smile most between seven and eight o'clock in the evening, we are cheeriest on Saturdays, and August is the happiest month.

It started me wondering … Between seven and eight in the evening we are likely to be at home with our family. Unless we work on Saturdays we are likely to spend it with our family. August is the last month of the Scottish summer holidays and the middle of the holidays in England in Wales, and we probably spend more time with our families during the holidays than any other time.

So could it be that families are what make us smile the most? I hope so – and I'm smiling at the very thought!

Sunday — **April 20**

THE EASTER DONKEY

I DID not know that morning
When I bore him into town,
How soon the loud hosannas
Would be changed to thorny crown.
I did not know that later
When I followed up the hill,
They'd nail Him upon a cross,
With suffering greater still.
And when I could not bear to watch
This strange, this cruel attack,
I turned and felt His shadow fall
Like balm upon my back.
And so it is that even now
All donkeys bear the sign:
A cross that is a testament
To show God's love divine.
Margaret Ingall

Monday — **April 21**

STRIVING for wealth and power may be all very well, as long as you use these qualities wisely. But for greater fulfilment in life, one more element needs to be included in these endeavours.

Four hundred years before Christ, Euripides observed: "It is a good thing to be rich and a good thing to be strong, but it is better to be loved of many friends."

How true that was – and still is!

Tuesday — **April 22**

THERE'S a very useful keyboard command those of us using laptops and other computers may be familiar with. It's Ctrl+Alt+Delete. If your computer freezes or gets stuck in a malfunctioning programme, pressing the Delete button while holding down the Control and Alternative buttons will usually reboot the system and help to solve the problem.

If only problems in life were so easy to deal with. If only you could Ctrl+Alt+Delete your way out of difficulties.

But maybe you can – if you "control" yourself, look around for an "alternative" and "delete" the situation.

Wednesday — **April 23**

THE Lady of the House had spent an evening with an old friend and arrived home with tears in her eyes. They had been to a cinema to see a revival of "The Railway Children" and both had been dabbing their eyes at the end when father and daughter were united again on the little railway platform.

It set me thinking about tears. We all shed them at times of sorrow, but there are other times when they come from sheer joy. Perhaps the sweetest tears of all are those we shed in sympathy with others, even if they are only make-believe characters on the silver screen.

Thursday — **April 24**

HOW often have you heard someone say: "He is only happy when he has something to moan about!"

Yes, we've probably all met one such Cheerful Charlie in our travels through life. President Abraham Lincoln summed it up nicely when he said, "Most folks are about as happy as they make their minds up to be."

How happy do you want to be? Resolve to be as happy as you can, and you'll probably succeed.

Friday — **April 25**

EVERY once in a while we hear tales of people who have had near-death experiences and claim to have visited Heaven. It's a comforting thought but no-one knows for sure whether such occurrences are real.

So how do we get to see Heaven in this life? The nineteeth century Dean of Westminster Arthur P. Stanley put it this way: "There are glimpses of heaven," he wrote, "in every act, or thought, or word that raises us above ourselves."

And until we arrive there to stay, it's a good way of visiting!

Saturday — **April 26**

WHAT difference can smiling make? Well, the writer Thomas Carlyle was a famously grumpy man. His wife, Jane, on the other hand was cheerful and devoted to her husband.

Writing to his mother, Carlyle expressed his appreciation and amazement that Jane loved him in a way which he was sure he didn't deserve. "She looks with such soft cheerfulness into my gloomy countenance," he wrote, "that new hope passes into me every time I meet her eye."

She did that with smiles. Now, who can we give new hope to today?

Sunday — **April 27**

" JUST don't ask, Francis," Marion said, forestalling my enquiry as to how she was. "Sorry, but it's been one of those days. I woke up feeling cross for no particular reason, then everything that could go wrong has gone wrong and, to crown it all, I've just had a difference of opinion on the phone with my good friend Katy.

"In fact," she added, "I'm about to take her flowers and apologise. Thank goodness she's so understanding."

As much as we may try, few of us manage to be saint-like every day. So let us emulate the words of Ephesians 4:32: "And be kind to one another, tender-hearted, forgiving each other, just as God in Christ has also forgiven you."

After all, no-one is perfect.

Monday — **April 28**

THERE is a little secret place
That leads down to a stream,
Where primroses and daffodils
In springtime blush unseen.
Where fairy-fingered foxgloves bloom
Their steeples straight and tall,
And buttercups and toadstools grow
Beside a crumbling wall.

As humble bees and butterflies
Sip nectar from the flowers,
The shy fish in the singing stream
Bask in the sunny hours.
It really seems quite magical
Though wild and overgrown,
For nature has endowed it with
A beauty all its own.
Kathleen Gillum

AFTERNOON IDYLL

Tuesday — **April 29**

WE all know that it's good to count our blessings, but I suspect we all know that sometimes it's easier said than done. Jill certainly found it hard to think of any positive aspects when the friend with whom she'd planned to go on holiday suddenly dropped out.

"When I realised I'd be spending the week alone, I felt really down," she said. "But the strange thing was that as soon as I decided to make the best of the situation, I found there were definite plus points.

"I was able to plan each day exactly as I wanted to without feeling selfish. It also meant I chatted to lots more people than I might have done. When I did return home, I found I'd gained confidence from knowing that I didn't have to rely on others to enjoy myself."

She laughed. "So you see, the more you look for blessings, the more you realise that they are all around you."

And that's a blessing in itself!

Wednesday — **April 30**

"MY garden's taught me many things," Harry said to me one sunny afternoon as he scattered seed on the bald patch of his lawn where his grandson's swing stood. "But mostly it's taught me how little I know. I've planted seeds and seedlings countless times and had grass, vegetables, fruit and flowers in return …"

He wiped his brow with the back of a hand and surveyed his garden with amazement before continuing: "But I couldn't even begin to understand how those everyday miracles work!"

Gertrude Jekyll, a garden designer born in the mid-1800s, would doubtless have stood alongside Harry and shared his wonder. She wrote: "A garden is a grand teacher. It teaches patience and careful watchfulness; it teaches industry and thrift; above all, it teaches entire trust."

May

THINGS LOVELY

HAVE you ever wondered at
The beauty of a tree,
The tiny velvet rosebud,
The humming fluffy bee?
The furry fledglings in the nest
And daisies small and shy,
A tinted sunset in the west,
A dainty butterfly.
Our world is full of wonder
There's beauty everywhere,
If only we would take the time
To stop – and stand – and stare.

Kathleen Gillum

DORIS was dismayed when they started to build a primary school on the fields behind her house. "You know how noisy children are when they're out playing," she said. "I'm dreading it."

Then she met a couple who live in the Hebrides off the Scottish coast. They told her how the older folk left in their community were missing the sound of children's laughter more than anything.

The school behind Doris is now open and she looks years younger. "I look forward to hearing the bell ringing for playtime," she said. "When the children run out, it's the happiest sound in the world."

Saturday — **May 3**

FOR Canadians, Tim Hortons coffee shops are well known – each day more than two and a half thousand outlets sell approximately four and a half million cups of coffee.

Tim Horton was a hockey hero who grew up poor in a northern Ontario mining town. He was so affected by poverty that he often worked in a gravel pit, even after he became a professional athlete.

Ron Joyce dropped out of high school at the age of sixteen and worked at various factory jobs, hoping somehow to make something of his life. Together Tim Horton and Ron Joyce founded their chain in the mid-1960s and through hard work and perseverance became two of the wealthiest businessmen in Canada.

In his memoirs, Ron Joyce quotes former U.S. President Calvin Coolidge:

"Nothing in the world can take the place of persistence. Talent will not; nothing is more common than unsuccessful men with talent. Genius will not; unrewarded genius is almost a proverb. Education alone will not; the world is full of educated derelicts. Persistence and determination alone are omnipotent."

Sunday — **May 4**

ACTS 20:35

IT'S better, so the Bible says,
To give than to receive;
And this, the more I see of life,
The more I do believe.
For happy is the chance to make
Another's life the brighter,
A double blessing for, you see,
It makes our own heart lighter.

Margaret Ingall

SAFE LANDING

Monday — **May 5**

HOW would you like to leave a mark on posterity? But surely that's for politicians, explorers, celebrities, you may say. How does the ordinary man or woman get to do the same?

Well, for some good advice on the subject the eighteenth century Swiss poet Johann Kaspar Lavater wrote these words: "Act well at the moment, and you have performed a good action for all eternity."

As easy as that! Now, choose your good deed – and make a good impression on forever.

Tuesday — **May 6**

I READ recently about the Celtic Christian hermits who went out to the remotest and wildest places in the 6th century AD to build chapels and to listen to God. They literally allowed their boats to be taken where God wanted.

What faith and courage! I think that today, in the 21st century, they can teach us a valuable lesson – sometimes we all need to find peace and quiet to listen, far away from other distractions.

Wednesday — **May 7**

ONE thing I enjoy doing more than almost anything – it costs nothing in money and next to nothing in effort – is passing on a compliment. If someone has something nice said about them, it is a pleasure to make sure they know about it!

Yorkshireman Henry Burton would surely have agreed, for after all it was he who, in the early 17th century, wrote these wise words:

"Did you hear the loving word? Pass it on. Like the singing of a bird? Pass it on. Let its music live and grow. Let it cheer another's woe. You have reaped what others sow. Pass it on."

Thursday — **May 8**

EVERY morning our old friend Mary likes to look for the woodpecker that comes to visit her feeder. All the other birds disappear when he flies in – even the robin ceases to look important.

This makes me smile as I am reminded of the pecking order we create as human beings. But we should keep in mind that God does not see us in those terms – we are all of equal worth in his eyes and that realisation is both a comfort and a joy.

Friday — **May 9**

HERE are some thoughts on what I'd call a celebration of friendship, the joy of having friends and being a friend to others.

Thomas Hughes wrote: "Blessed are they who have the gift of making friends for it is one of God's best gifts." The nineteeth-century American natural history writer David Henry Thoreau believed "the most I can do for my friend is simply to be his friend."

Friendship enhances our lives and gladdens our hearts.

Saturday — **May 10**

THERE'S an old saying about the indispensable man. "Clasp both hands together and put them in a bucket of water," it goes. "Then draw them out again. The hole you leave in the water is a measure of how hard it will be to replace you."

At the mention of this our friend John laughed and turned the phrase around. "Ah, but while my hands are filling that space, the water doesn't have to!" he said.

"I know lots of folk could help my neighbours, do what I do for my family, be there for my friends. I'm just glad they don't have to and that I get the chance to. I'm not indispensable," he said with a laugh. "I'm grateful!"

Sunday — **May 11**

"OH, dear – decisions, decisions ..." Josie smiled ruefully as she deliberated over what sort of biscuits to buy. "I do wish I could be more positive. Heaven help me when it comes to making the really important choices in life!"

Josie may have been making light of her indecision, but in fact her words can be taken quite literally. I suspect every one of us knows how hard it can feel to be faced with a truly difficult decision, but remember, we don't have to do it alone.

"Trust in the Lord with all your heart, and don't lean on your own understanding. In all things acknowledge him, and he shall direct your way."

That's what it says in Proverbs 3: 5-6 – wise words for us all to remember.

Monday — **May 12**

RECENTLY I was reading about ten lost and abandoned owls being cared for at Tiggywinkles Wildlife Hospital near Aylesbury. Some had been orphaned when their parents were killed, while others had fallen out of their nests. The orphans came from different locations in Buckinghamshire, so none were related and they were to be released back into the wild when fully grown.

A Tiggywinkles staff member said that the owls had formed a really close family. Photographs showed them sitting together in a row, enjoying each other's company and life in the hospital's aviary.

I couldn't help but reflect that the tiny birds beautifully complement these words from Dr Phil McGraw: "There is an interconnectedness among members that bonds the family, much like mountain climbers who rope themselves together when climbing a mountain, so that if someone should slip or need support, he's held up by the others until he regains his footing."

BONNIE BANKS

Tuesday — **May 13**

CHRISTINA ROSSETTI, in her poem "A Dumb Friend", likened human friendship to her binding attachment to an evergreen tree which she had planted when both were young. From her window she had watched it grow and weather the seasons over many years.

She had sat beneath its protective, shady boughs, watched its movements in the "tender winds" and "rattling gale", and noted its ageing when "silvered by the frost". This "faithful pleasant friend" now towered above her, and grew, she wrote, with her growth and was strengthened by her strength and, without speaking: "It seems a very friend to me, in all my secrets wise."

Strong and silent friends, like the tree, are reliably ever present to share both fortune and misfortune, as I was reminded by Mark Rutherford's words about his friends: "It is always the unspoken, the unconscious, which is their reality to me." Roberta Israeloff remarked: "Silences and distances are woven into the texture of every true friendship."

Wednesday — **May 14**

THE Lady of the House didn't quite understand when her friend Ella put her nail varnish brush back into its container and told her that she felt sorry for her poor right hand. Being right handed, she explained, her right hand generally did more work than the left. It also made an elegant job of painting the nails on her left hand.

The left hand, being less used, made a rather clumsy job of the nails on the right hand.

"And it's usually the same in life," Ella said. "Whenever you see someone looking immaculate and appearing like they could do a lot of stuff, search beyond them for the slightly shabbier and harder-working soul who made them look so good. And say thank you to them!"

Something for us all to think about today.

Thursday — **May 15**

MICHAEL and June were treating themselves to a well-deserved café lunch when the Lady of the House bumped into them.

"We've just had our niece and her little boys to stay with us for a few days," June explained. "And even though it's been tiring, it's been magical to see life through the eyes of children. Even something as simple as a spider's web or a dandelion takes on a whole new meaning. In fact, we've both decided that we'll try to keep that attitude, instead of just taking things for granted."

As Walt Streightiff once observed: "There are no seven wonders of the world in the eyes of a child. There are seven million."

And who wouldn't want to be a wonder-millionaire?

Friday — **May 16**

OUR friend Cassandre often posts her thoughts on social networking sites. Growing up in Haiti, she has witnessed many hardships and challenges yet she is one of the most positive and inspiring people you could ever meet.

One day she wrote these words online: "Feeling gratitude and not expressing it is like wrapping a present and not giving it."

What a beautiful way to approach each day!

Saturday — **May 17**

HOW would you like to be able to do the impossible? Well, according to the seventeenth-century fable writer Jean De La Fontaine nothing was. He wrote: "Man is so made that when anything fires his soul, impossibilities vanish."

So, if you want to achieve more than you ever thought you could, first find out what fires your soul. That might not be easy – but it won't be impossible!

Sunday — **May 18**

DENNIS QUAID, the star of films like "The Day After Tomorrow" and "The Big Easy", is a man whose maturity was accompanied by faith and a better standard of behaviour. Now he is what he likes to call a fix-it dad.

But when the twin babies he and his wife had tried so hard for were in intensive care he had to recognise this wasn't something he could fix. Years later he is convinced that the prayers of his family and fans saved his children.

As he said, "I'm still a fix-it dad, even though I know there are many things that I won't be able to fix. Those times I have to trust in a higher power, the ultimate fix-it dad, the Father whose abiding love is spelled out pretty clearly in the story of the prodigal son."

"'My son,' the father said, 'you are always with me, and everything I have is yours.'" (Luke 15:31)

Monday — **May 19**

OUR friend Edith recently bought a skirt that was a perfect fit at the waist and just the colour she wanted, but was a few inches too long. When she took it to the dressmaker's to be adjusted, she noticed a poster on the wall featuring this quote by Oscar Wilde: "One should either be a work of art, or wear a work of art." Well said, indeed!

Tuesday — **May 20**

"TUESDAYS With Morrie" is a moving story about Professor Morrie Schwartz and a former student. The bestseller, published in 1997 and later made into a film, brims with the wisdom and lessons Morrie shares during visits in the final stage of his life.

As Morrie put it so beautifully: "The most important thing in this world is to learn to give out love, and let it come in."

A truth that will always light our path, don't you agree?

Wednesday — **May 21**

ELBERT HUBBARD, the nineteeth-century American author and editor, once said: "One can endure sorrow alone, but it takes two to be glad." We will all experience sadness at some time in our life, but we often prefer not to burden others with it.

However, the opposite, being glad, is an emotion we must enjoy with a partner or friend to give it its true worth. So let's all resolve to share some of that precious happiness today!

Thursday — **May 22**

THERE is a passage in Anthony Trollope's "Barchester Chronicles" which I always find touching. The daughter of Rev Harding says to her father: "May I travel with you, father?"

His reply is: "You always travel with me, my dear."

A few simple words, but such a wealth of feeling and love. Isn't this the way we feel about those we love, but often find it difficult to explain? They are always close to us in heart and mind. Whatever the distance or circumstances, we always travel together.

Friday — **May 23**

BARGAIN BUY!

I GOT myself a stylish coat,
A super bargain buy,
And hoped, parading down the street,
I'd catch an envious eye!
Amid the crowds, a voice I knew,
Called after me to shout:
"I know you've been to the jumble sale –
That's the coat I threw out!"
                    Elizabeth Gozney

Saturday — **May 24**

HAVE you noticed how a seemingly ordinary day can have unexpected moments of beauty and serenity?

One afternoon, on our way to the shops, the Lady of the House and I passed a group of primary school pupils on an outing with their teacher. It was a great adventure for them; on a nearby wall a white cat could be seen sunning itself contentedly. Suddenly I remembered these words by Pam Brown:

"Between the house and the store there are little pockets of happiness. A bird, a garden, a friend's greeting, a child's smile, a cat in the sunshine needing a stroke. Recognise them – or ignore them. It's always up to you."

We all need to slow down at times and find these "pockets of happiness."

Sunday — **May 25**

HOPE FOR THE WEEK

THE Lord will be my lantern
To lead me through the week,
To show the way when days are dark
And light the path I seek.

And when the shadows gather
Or hover round my door,
His light will lift and warm my heart
And give me hope once more.

The Lord will be my lantern
Through any stress or strife,
And guide me always, day by day,
Each week throughout my life.
Iris Hesselden

Monday — **May 26**

SIR FRANK CRISP, 1st Baronet (1843-1919) was a lawyer and writer. He lived at Friar Park in Henley on Thames.

Years later, in 1970, the late George Harrison of Beatles fame bought Friar Park as his home. George used some of Crisp's quotes, which were engraved in various locations at Friar Park, as inspiration for songs. One example advises: "Scan not a friend with a microscopic glass. You know his faults, now let his foibles pass."

A valuable lesson in friendship, wouldn't you agree?

Tuesday — **May 27**

"THE great thing about being on holiday," observed Maggie, who had just returned from a long seaside break, "is that it's so much easier to live in the moment. I mean, because I've consciously been looking around, enjoying new experiences, I simply haven't had the time to worry about all the niggling little things that don't actually matter that much, anyway."

This makes me think we should try a little harder to live in the moment. So I'm going to try to keep that holiday feeling whether or not I actually am away from home!

Wednesday — **May 28**

IN many homes a lot of household jobs get done to the cheerful accompaniment of the radio, so I wasn't surprised to hear our neighbour's handyman humming along to the song: "Oh Lord, won't you buy me a Mercedes Benz?"

"That song always makes me laugh," Rob chuckled. "It's just so typical of the way we long for things we don't need, yet completely forget to ask for the really important things in life that have nothing to do material possessions."

Next time we hear that song, it will be a good reminder of things that actually are worth asking for!

LEAN ON ME

Thursday — **May 29**

WHAT'S the first thing you think of in the morning? Well, if you're lucky, you are a naturally buoyant person who greets the day with cheerfulness and optimism.

If, however, you find it harder to be quite so positive, consider the words of someone who must have had his fair share of concerns. The Roman Emperor Marcus Aurelius said, "When you arise in the morning, think of what a precious privilege it is to be alive – to breathe, to think, to enjoy, to love."

It's a thought that may help you to conquer the world!

Friday — **May 30**

ARE you facing a particular challenge today? I suspect most of us will, whether it's a major physical or mental hurdle, or something so minor that we can manage to take it in our stride. So here are a couple of thoughts to encourage you:

"It always seems impossible until it's done."   Nelson Mandela

And – as it's inevitable our efforts cannot always be entirely successful, here is a parting thought from Carol Burnett:

"I have always grown from my problems and challenges; from the things that don't work out, that's when I've really learned."

Good luck!

Saturday — **May 31**

*H*OW can one say "thank you" for such a world as ours?
The mountains and the meadows, the forests and the flowers,
The snowflakes and the starlight, the seas and shining sand,
No world could be more wondrous, no gift more vast or grand,
So how to show our gladness? What ways to best employ?
The best and finest "thank you" is simply to – enjoy!

Margaret Ingall

June

Sunday — **June 1**

OUR friend John was surprisingly energetic when I bumped into him one day. He explained he'd been at a church fund-raiser in a nearby village the night before. At the end of a very successful evening, somehow or other, he had been left with the task of clearing everything away.

"Actually, Walter and I took care of it," he explained. Now, I know Walter is a very quiet man with various health problems, so surely he wouldn't have been much help moving tables and such like?

"That's where you'd be wrong," John said with a grin. "As I finished stacking the last of the chairs, Walter, who'd been sitting to one side, surveyed the hall. He nodded slowly and smiled – just a little – as if he was thinking, a good job, well done."

"Was that all?" I asked.

"All?" retorted John. "It was plenty. I may have done all the lifting, but it was Walter who did the up-lifting!"

"Therefore encourage one another and build each other up, just as in fact you are doing." (Thessalonians 1 5:11)

Monday — **June 2**

ARTHUR RUBINSTEIN, born in Lodz in Poland in 1887, became famous worldwide as one of Europe's greatest pianists. He lived a long and busy life, meeting people of many nationalities.

He once said: "Love life and life will love you back. Love people and they will love you back."

Isn't that a fine thought to pass on to friends today?

Tuesday — **June 3**

THE Lady of the House and I have two friends who love to visit old churches in Europe. On one occasion when in Brussels they visited a church in the middle of a busy shopping precinct, a haven of tranquillity among the crowds. There, they picked up a leaflet in French which was headed *Temps de Vacances* (holiday time) and it read as follows:

Take time to play, it is the secret of everlasting youth.
Take time to read, it is the source of knowledge.
Take time to love, and to be loved, it is a grace from God.
Take time to make friends, it is the way to happiness.
Take time to laugh, it is the music of the soul.
Take time to think, it is the source of all things done.
Take time to give, life is too short to be selfish.
Take time to work, it is the price of success.

Now, don't you think that this is good advice, not only for holidays, but for everyday life as well?

Wednesday — **June 4**

NO-ONE can choose what happens to them in life, but we can choose how we deal with it. These words may be a bit of a cliché, but they sprang to mind when I read an interview with Pam Warren, a survivor of the Paddington rail crash of 1999.

The accident turned her world upside down. For months she had to wear a plastic mask to help heal her terrible burns, while the psychological and practical effects threatened to mar her life for ever.

But Pam is a determined lady and won through against all the odds. Nowadays, as a resolute rail safety campaigner, she is no longer afraid to travel. "I'm just going to slap a big smile on my face, have a go at everything, and talk to anyone who'll talk to me," she says.

What an admirable attitude! And how rich our lives would be if we all embraced that philosophy.

Thursday — **June 5**

THE poet Hafiz once wrote: "How did the rose ever open its heart and give to this world all of its beauty? It felt the encouragement of light against its being."

In this world we can all be the rose that gifts the world with beauty, or we can be the light of encouragement that makes the gift possible.

Friday — **June 6**

IT'S my birthday tomorrow," young Jack told me one day, his face glowing with excitement. "I'm going to be nine and I can't wait!"

His grandmother smiled at me and said: "I do wish I could feel that keen about my own birthday next month. I must admit that as the years go by, I approach them with resignation rather than enthusiasm."

It's not an uncommon attitude, but before we allow ourselves to get too gloomy, it's worth remembering what Francis Bacon said: "Age appears best in four things: old wood to burn, old wine to drink, old friends to trust and old authors to read."

You see, there are benefits to ageing that we don't even see until we get there.

Saturday — **June 7**

LAUGHTER is important to each and every one of us. It helps to bring out the sunshine on many a cloudy day and today I'd like to share with you one of my favourite quotations from Mort Walker on the subject:

"Laughter is the brush that sweeps away the cobwebs of the heart."

I hope there will always be room for laughter in your life and may it give you joy to share with others.

Sunday — **June 8**

ON a website where people share kind deeds and encouragement someone had posted this online: "I've just called a friend to let her know I've seen the first humming birds arrive so that she can put her feeders out in the garden."

So she made a phone call, and her friend put feeders out, but the hummingbirds would know nothing of any of this, of course. All those amazing little creatures would know was that, once again, plentiful food had been provided.

We are like those hummingbirds in that most of us don't know half of what goes into the blessings we receive – but still they keep arriving!

"'So then, don't be afraid. I will provide for you and your children.' And he reassured them and spoke kindly to them."

(Genesis 50:21)

Monday — **June 9**

OUR friend Helen has her own unique way of signing letters and greeting cards. It is a short and simple message, but one certain to touch the heart of all who receive it: *Love and Rainbows.*

These words rather sum up what we need in life. Love to keep us strong, whatever our circumstances, and a rainbow, now and then, to give us fresh hope. If you have a wish for family and friends, perhaps you would like to add these three words next time you get in touch by post.

May they fill your days and light your life!

Tuesday — **June 10**

TROUBLES can be defined by how we look at them. They might stop us in our tracks or we might take the advice of a philosopher who said: "This mountain was not placed in front of you to defeat you – but to show you what great heights you can rise to!"

Wednesday — **June 11**

" **I** 'VE noticed it before," said the Lady of the House. "It's a feeling that's hard to explain, but sometimes when I'm listening to music or reading a good book, or just enjoying being in beautiful surroundings, it's almost like a kind of recognition – a realisation that something just feels completely right."

I understood what she was trying to say and, like her, I think it's an awareness that can be found in all sorts of different ways. Harold Kushner, for example, once said: "When you carry out acts of kindness you get a wonderful feeling inside. It's as though something inside your body responds and says, yes, this is how I ought to feel."

It's perhaps the best way to achieve that most satisfying sensation.

Thursday — **June 12**

A N old proverb tells us: "If ever you need a helping hand – you'll find one on the end of your arm!" It's a witty and useful reminder that we can usually help ourselves.

But there's another way of looking at it. That thing on the end of our arm can still be a help for others even when we don't need one. It's too "handy" to let go to waste.

Friday — **June 13**

N OT far from where our friend Patrick lives is a community centre which provides support and resources for adults with disabilities. A sign outside announces future events and workshops.

One day he noticed that someone had used the sign to share these thought-provoking words:

Everyone is hungry for a kind word. Feed them.
Certainly a worthy challenge to consider today – or any day of the week.

Saturday — **June 14**

FUGITIVES

THEY'RE ruthlessly rooted from borders,
And never allowed into tubs,
In fact, they're persona non grata
In all horticultural clubs.
And so, in a way, they are outlaws,
Unwelcome, unloved and reviled,
Rejected by civilisation
They have to survive in the wild.

And yet, these humble outsiders
Have powers both potent and real,
And those who are wise to their secrets
May use them to soothe and to heal.
For now they brighten the byways,
Lighting the earth with their glow;
Where'er a dark corner needs dusting with gold
Be sure dandelions will grow.

Tricia Sturgeon

Sunday — **June 15**

IN Ancient Greece theatre tragedies were generally four-act plays and, of course, everything went wrong in the last act. Comedies, though, had five acts, and everything turned out well in the fifth act, leaving both audience and cast contented and happy.

You could say that a year is split into four acts – spring, summer, autumn and winter. If our lives were to follow the same pattern, as they so often seem to, they might well be described as tragedies. But, thankfully, we have the promise of more up above, where everything will turn out for the best.

"And the Lord shall deliver me from every evil work, and will preserve me unto his heavenly kingdom: to whom be glory for ever and ever. Amen." (Timothy II 4:18)

Monday — **June 16**

OUR old friend Mary has a stock of pithy and wise sayings that she first heard from her mother. If she pulled a face when something displeased her, her mother would warn: "The wind will change, and you'll stay like that!"

If she came in tired and frustrated from tackling some difficult job outside, Mary recalls that her mother would comment: "These jobs always take longer than you think." If something special like a small cake had to be divided in two, she would say: "You cut and she will choose!"

Even now, when trying to polish her shoes with a quick rub before dashing off to the shops, Mary says that she can almost hear her mother calling out: "You can't clean your shoes on your feet!"

Mothers, take heart – your words are never lost.

Tuesday — **June 17**

A NEW art gallery had opened and Peter and Laura decided to spend an afternoon there. They wandered through the various exhibition areas, enjoying the work of local artists. Later, when they were almost ready to leave, they noticed something that could easily have been missed.

Framed and placed among a collection of landscape watercolours was this quote by Mark Twain: "Kindness is the language which the deaf can hear and blind can see."

Words worth exhibiting, indeed.

Wednesday — **June 18**

HAVE you been putting off writing that difficult letter? Or perhaps you have been intending to help a friend or call on a neighbour. Well, the German poet Goethe once gave this advice:

"What you can do, or dream you can do – begin it. Boldness has genius, power and magic in it."

Thursday — **June 19**

WHEN did your postman last deliver to you a handwritten letter from a friend? In today's world of mobile phones, e-mail and the Internet, we can communicate almost instantly with friends and relatives across the globe.

However, none of these will ever be the same as receiving a handwritten letter, which you can keep, perhaps treasure, and re-read as often as you wish. There is something about the feel of a sheet of writing paper and matching envelope, or an illustrated notelet, with a friend's personal writing style, that electronic communication can never compete with.

So, instead of picking up the phone or logging on to your computer, take a few minutes to write a letter with that fountain pen hiding at the back of your bureau. The trouble you have taken and your thoughtfulness will be greatly appreciated. And you can enjoy a walk in the fresh air to the post-box!

Friday — **June 20**

WE DAY is a powerful movement of young people leading local and global change. An initiative of Free The Children, We Day harnesses the energy and passion of a young community of change makers to show them they can make a difference.

In packed stadiums, We Day explores the social issues of today and provides ways in which everyone can find a place within the movement to create global change.

Hundreds of thousands of people have attended since the first event was held in 2007. In the 2010/2011 school year, participants volunteered more than 1.7 million hours of their time, raised 5.4 million dollars in donations to support local and global organisations, and collected more than 519,000 pounds of food to stock food banks.

Through We Day, participants learn that it is worthwhile to care.

Saturday — **June 21**

OUR young friend Marc was telling us that skateboarding enthusiasts around the world celebrate the spirit of this exhilarating activity every year on June 21. Hundreds of thousands gather, he told us, on this day to hop on a skateboard and participate in numerous exciting events held all over the world.

For example, in Afghanistan, skateboarders took to Kabul's streets in the only Afghan public sports event with all ages and nationalities taking part together. Since the event was first held in 2009, the number of skateboarders has increased from forty to one hundred and eighty. The universal ability of this day to unite people for a cause or a just-for-fun event has been gratifying for the organisers.

World Skateboarding Day is not only a celebration of the sport, but also a way to raise funds for the community, work together and make new friends.

Sunday — **June 22**

A SUNDAY PRAYER

ANOTHER week beginning, Lord,
Who knows what it will bring,
Will there be light and laughter,
And days when hope takes wing?

Or will there be a sadness, Lord,
For things we left behind,
A path that's rough and often steep
And sometimes hard to find?

No matter what the week may hold
Whatever comes along,
Please wrap us always in Your love
And keep us safe and strong.
                              Iris Hesselden

Monday — **June 23**

SEVERAL months ago the company our friend Ron worked for underwent restructuring and he lost his job. It was quite a shock after more than twenty years, but from the outset he decided to make the best of the situation. He made up his mind to start each new day with three favourite things – a freshly-brewed cup of tea, a silent prayer and a long walk – before tackling the rest of the day.

Then one afternoon he came across these charming words by author Anais Nin. In just a sentence, she had eloquently captured the wonder of life's simplest pleasures:

"A leaf fluttered in through the window this morning, as if supported by the rays of the sun, a bird settled on the fire escape, joy in the task of coffee, joy accompanied me as I walked."

Contentment can arrive in the most unexpected ways, don't you agree? And just last week I heard that Ron has found a new job, one which will suit him far better than his previous post.

Tuesday — **June 24**

EARTH is now home to seven billion people so it is becoming harder to find places in which you can be alone, if solitude is what you seek. It is also good for your inner self to have your own secret place where you can be content within your own mind for a time, shutting out the more challenging aspects of life.

Solitude and silence are the ingredients for reflecting on your own circumstances, and you should enjoy these precious times. Me-time is not selfishness – it can bring freedom and healing, whether in the great outdoors, in the quiet of a church or your own little corner in a café.

Try awarding yourself some me-time when life starts to get on top of you. It is fine to be alone – you owe it to yourself from time to time. Why not try it today?

IN MEMORIAM

A LA MÉMOIRE DE
THOMAS DE CARTERET DE LA VAUROQUE

Wednesday — **June 25**

ROSE likes to time her early morning dog walks to coincide with the breaking of dawn. She calls them her "beholding walks," when she sees the world as God saw it when He made it out of the darkness – "and, behold, it was very good."

The word "behold" is an old English one, meaning to see something, usually something wonderful. But it also implies holding on to something and I'm sure Rose holds the pleasures of her walks firmly in her heart.

Now, wouldn't it be wonderful if we could expand her idea and make our whole lives one long beholding walk?

Thursday — **June 26**

MAKE IT HAPPEN

THE moment that you think "I can't,"
Replace it with "I can,"
Keep trying till your goal's achieved,
Don't be an "also ran."

Be certain, do not hesitate
To stick to what is right,
But find the art of compromise,
For all's not black or white.

Be positive in all your thoughts,
Don't let them go astray,
Nor let words like "I don't know how"
Intrude, get in the way.

Rely upon the power of God,
Let fulfilment take wing,
Then armed with confidence and hope,
You'll deal with everything.
                                    Chrissy Greenslade

Friday — **June 27**

OFTEN see Adrian when I'm out walking. He's an elderly gentleman, who loves to ride his bicycle despite being well over eighty.

Every time he passes me, he calls out some sort of cheery greeting or encouragement. One grey day that threatened a downpour at any moment, he called out: "We won't get wet! We'll get home just before the storm for a nice cup of tea!"

And on a blazing hot summer's afternoon that made walking and keeping cool difficult, he stopped, took out a handkerchief to mop his face and quipped, "The sun is doing a fine job today, making sure everything grows!"

Such exchanges always leave me feeling uplifted, for Adrian's words are filled with a simple, glad appreciation for everything around him. Wouldn't it be wonderful if we could all pass on a little cheer each day just like him?

Saturday — **June 28**

LOVE my garden but I know that not everyone is lucky enough to have one. Our young friend Alex lives in a flat and his family doesn't even have a window box to brighten up the day.

I was at a loss for words when he leaned over our garden fence one afternoon and said, "Ask me what I'm growing these days!"

I ventured that he might be growing taller, or growing his hair longer. He rolled his eyes at my feeble response and, in return, shared this quotation:

"The heart is like a garden," he quoted. "It can grow compassion or fear, resentment or love. What seeds will you plant there?"

"Well, I'm growing compassion and love," he told me as he waved and went on his way.

I looked back at our little patch and realised you don't need a garden to grow beauty.

Sunday — **June 29**

IN India, more than two million children under the age of five die each year, mostly from malnutrition and hypothermia.

For Stanford MBA student Jane Chen and three other Stanford graduate students, these grim statistics provided a very real opportunity to demonstrate God's love and compassion. They worked together to design a baby wrap product for a class challenge in 2008 – Jane wanted to do even more. She co-founded Embrace, a non-profit organisation that distributes the innovative wrap and saves thousands of infant lives in Third-World countries.

The team has moved to India to dedicate their lives to this cause. During the next few years, Embrace expects to reach more than a million babies around the world, a considerable achievement.

"He has dispersed abroad, he has given to the poor; his righteousness endures forever; his horn will be exalted with honour." (Psalms 112:9)

Monday — **June 30**

JAMES powered up the hill on his way to a busy day.
"We need a rest," said the man with the old sheepdog at his feet. He was leaning on a fence looking back at the way James had come.

"Well, we all do from time to time," replied James as he hurried on by. It occurred to him that the next time he would take a rest would be when he lay in bed that night.

On a notion, he turned and saw what the other fellow saw – fields sweeping away towards the distant misty hills and a million acres of sky still tinged with the dawn. Then he realised that he'd only seen the path in front of his feet since he'd left the house. He'd missed everything else.

Next time, he decided, he would follow his new friend's example and raise his sights from the busy day. Maybe by taking a rest James would see … the rest.

BLUE HORIZON

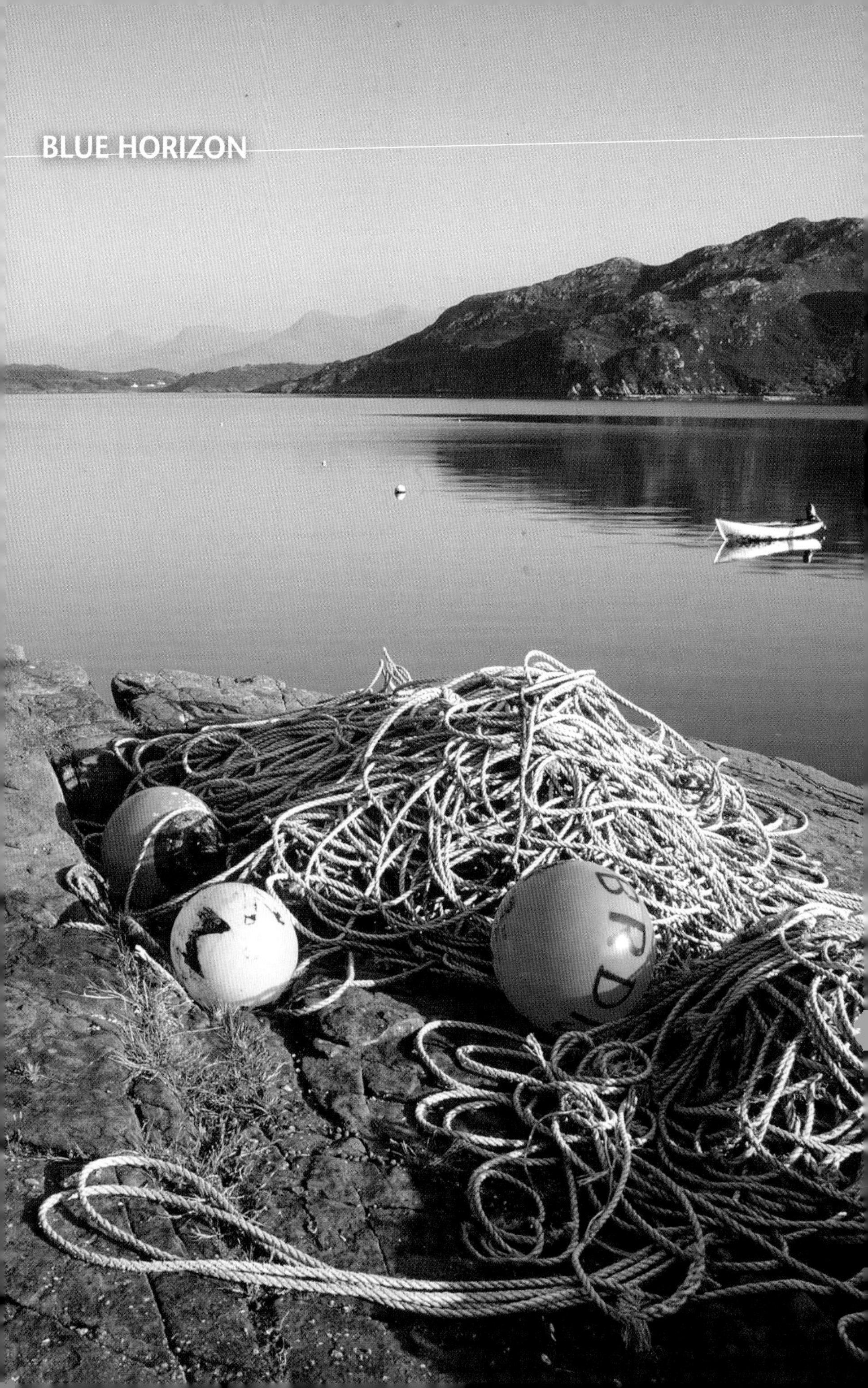

July

Tuesday — **July 1**

POWER. What does it mean to you? No, I'm not talking about the current that comes from the electric sockets on your wall. Is it having the ear of presidents and prime ministers? Or is it when you own a business empire?

Well, I prefer the definition offered by Brooke Astor, the philanthropist. Putting it at its very simplest and its most wonderful, she observed: "Power is the ability to do good things for others."

Wednesday — **July 2**

FAITHFUL PET

YOU'VE always been a faithful pet
And dearest friend to me,
We've spent much time together
You've kept me company.
We'd go out for our daily walks
By river, field and lake,
And meet so many folk we knew
Upon the route we'd take.

Whilst I was doing all my chores
You would just romp and play,
And bark at all the passers-by
In your own friendly way.
We really are the best of pals
As anyone can see,
My loved companion, special pet
You're very dear to me.

Kathleen Gillum

Thursday — **July 3**

I WAS chatting with Geoff before he arrived at his work. As he turned to leave he said, "Well, I'm off to bring some more clarity into the world!"

No, he's neither a philosopher nor a clergyman. He's a window cleaner.

Each of us, no matter what we do for a living, can make the day a brighter one by following Geoff's example and doing what we do with a sparkling attitude.

Friday — **July 4**

N OW, I have spent many a summer's afternoon in the garden enjoying the company of flowers. But I don't think I ever saw them quite the way the preacher Henry Ward Beecher did.

"Flowers have an expression of countenance as much as men or animals," he wrote. "Some seem to smile, some have a sad expression; some are pensive and diffident; others again are plain, honest and upright, like the broad-faced sunflower or the hollyhock."

Now I can't help but wonder what the flowers would be thinking if they were people – and which of my friends are most like which of my flowers.

Saturday — **July 5**

T HE publisher William Randolph Hearst was so impressed by the work one of his columnists was doing that he offered him six months paid holiday as a reward. The columnist, Arthur Brisbane, declined for two reasons.

"The first," he explained, "is that if I stop writing my column for half a year it might affect the circulation of your newspapers. The second reason is that it might not!"

Let's make sure that if we took six months off from being us, people would definitely miss us.

Sunday — **July 6**

ENJOYING a drive in Somerset with cliffs towering majestically up to the Mendip Heights on one side and the Cheddar Gorge on the other, Janet and Barry spotted an ideal place for a picnic, a small, grassy area on one side of the road where two tall rocks were split, quite close together.

Janet began to unpack their picnic and when the sun disappeared behind dark clouds she glanced up at the threatening sky. As she looked down again, she caught sight of a plaque.

It said that the Rev. Augustus M. Toplady was out riding in the rocky terrain of Burrington Combe when he was taken unawares by a sudden violent storm. Taking shelter in the space between two rocks he waited, and while there, words came into his mind.

He searched for something on which to write them down and caught sight of a playing card on the ground. The young man picked it up and was able to write the first few lines of his inspiring hymn:

Rock of Ages, cleft for me
Let me hide myself in Thee . . .

Studying these majestic rocks with just enough space in between to shelter a man, Janet thought of the words she had read in Psalms 61:3 – "For thou hast been a shelter for me, and a strong tower from the enemy."

Monday — **July 7**

I HAVE been pondering over some words of G.K. Chesterton, a popular writer and wit last century. "The way to love something," he wrote, "is to realise that it might be lost."

It's so true. We should care for the good and the beautiful, tend and nurture it. Whatever it is – our countryside, the birds of the air, our towns and villages. They need all the love and care we can give them so that future generations can know and love them, too.

Tuesday — **July 8**

CAMERON was excited about his newly-acquired driver's licence. However, as a young and inexperienced driver, he had a lot to learn, as he was soon to find out. After a mishap with his mother's car, he considered fudging the facts when she asked for an explanation about a dent in the front passenger door.

Sensing her son's hesitation, his mother said gently, "Never forget that a lie can circle the globe before truth can lace up its shoes."

Words to live by, indeed!

Wednesday — **July 9**

A HOLY PLACE

I WILL make my spot on earth
A holy place.
When the weeds of worry grow,
Twisting and choking,
I will water them with trust.
When stark, black branches of fear
Clatter eerily,
I will grace them with the greenery of faith.
When anger tears a dark, gaping hole
Across the road,
I will fill it with forgiveness and keep walking
Without looking back.
I will plant
Seedlings of charity
And integrity
And invite all who pass by my spot on earth
To rest beneath their shade,
And be refreshed
In this humble, holy place.

Rachel Wallace-Oberle

Thursday — **July 10**

" **I** WAS in such a rush yesterday," Evelyn told me. "I'd already done lots of shopping, and I was hurrying home where I had even more jobs waiting for me. And then I saw the butterfly...

"It was such a pretty thing that I couldn't help but pause and watch it skimming from flower to flower, dancing in the sunshine. By the time it finally disappeared, I had come to see that chores really aren't the most important thing in life."

It was poet John Masefield who once described butterflies as "the souls of summer hours", which makes me feel sure that he, too, saw them as reminders of something far bigger and beautiful.

Sometimes it's the small things that give us the best sense of perspective.

Friday — **July 11**

W HEN Angela told her best friend Susan that her parents were planning to emigrate to New Zealand, both young girls were heartbroken. Promising to write, Susan was taken to the dockside to wave farewell, and then she went home and picked up her pen . . .

Soon their letters were regularly crossing the vast distance between them. News of school events, boyfriends, weddings, children and, eventually, grandchildren followed over several decades. Nowadays email is often their method of keeping in touch, but the link between them has never been broken.

"We lead very different lifestyles, and yet I still think of Angela as one of my closest companions," Susan said. "That's no mean achievement for someone who lives so far away!"

I once heard it said that true friendship is when two friends can walk in opposite directions yet remain side by side. Truly Angela and Susan – and many others like them – are living testament of the power of friendship to overcome all odds.

SWEET MOMENTS

HOW wonderful is nature
As she sets for us the scene
Of lakes and woods and waterfalls,
Rolling hills and glorious greens.
The scent of summer flowers,
Showers shining in the sun
Is balm upon the spirit
And beauty newly spun.
How wonderful a crashing sea
To pound upon the shore
The roller-coaster wanton waves
Where seagulls screech and soar.
How wonderful these images
Friends forever new
Take time out, reflect, rejoice,
Our lovely world welcomes you.

Dorothy McGregor

Sunday — **July 13**

JENNIFER had intended to have a thorough clear-out of her cupboards, but soon became happily distracted by the discovery of a pile of diaries dating back to her childhood.

"One of the things that struck me most," she told the Lady of the House, "was the way Sundays have changed. They used to be so much quieter when I was young. Yet despite all the differences, I still find them special and different.

"I love having the opportunity to reflect on the past week, the chance to think about future plans and, best of all, the time to slow down and appreciate just what a wonderful world it is. In fact, I agree with what Longfellow said: 'Sunday is the golden clasp that binds together the volume of the week'."

She laughed. "And, you know, perhaps that includes all those volumes of my diaries as well."

Monday — **July 14**

NOT long ago, our friend John attended a family reunion. Loved ones he hadn't seen for many years came from all parts of the world to spend a weekend together. It was a joyous time filled with lots of laughter, good food and many treasured memories.

Here are some inspiring thoughts to share with you today on what it means to be part of a family:

"You don't choose your family. They are God's gift to you, as you are to them."
Desmond Tutu

"Rejoice with your family in the beautiful land of life!"
Albert Einstein

"If the family were a fruit, it would be an orange, a circle of sections, held together but separable – each segment distinct."
Letty Cottin Pogrebin

Tuesday — **July 15**

IF one candle lights another, they both shine brightly with no loss of light. Some centuries ago, the Duke of Urbino in Italy took the thought a bit further and made it his family coat of arms. His shield bore a lit candle from which others could be lit. The Latin motto *Non Degener Addam* meant "I add without loss."

Making things better without costing anything, adding without taking away, what a lovely way to live a life. What a wonderful lesson from the humble candle!

Wednesday — **July 16**

HERE are three thoughts about failure – but remember, just one could lead you to success:

Keep on trying. It's better to be a Has-Been than a Never-Will-Be.
There is no failure except in failing to try again.
If you try, you might. If you don't, you won't!

LOOK!

Thursday — **July 17**

HAVE you ever been so annoyed with someone that you found yourself thinking they just weren't worth bothering with? Novelist Willa Cather had an interesting take on the subject.

"Sometimes a fellow we have disliked for a lifetime for his arrogance and conceit lets fall a single commonplace word that shows us another side, another man really; a man uncertain, puzzled, and in the dark like ourselves," she observed.

Everyone has something about them that is worth appreciating, no matter how hard they try to hide it.

Friday — **July 18**

THE yellow daisy had been plucked and then discarded. It lay on the rain-washed tarmac and seemed to have been stepped on more than once. But its colour still had something of the sunshine in it and the smooth, delicate curves, leading to the tips of each perfectly spaced petal, were natural, mathematical poetry.

Even in its time of trial the daisy was beautiful enough to stop me in my tracks. And I thought how blessed I was to know several people just like that little flower.

Saturday — **July 19**

WHEN it comes to doing good there are always plenty of reasons not to make the effort, it seems. When it comes to helping someone it is sometimes tempting to find some aspect of that person that might make them seem not worth helping.

But let us keep in mind that there is no situation that cannot be made better and no man or woman who does not yearn for love and kindness.

So next time you are deciding whether to help or not, bear in mind the old African proverb: "For the sake of the rose the thorn is watered."

Sunday — **July 20**

SEVENTH DAY

AND on the seventh day, it's said
Our Lord beheld the world He'd made
Rejoiced in all that He surveyed,
From sun, to sea, to tree, to glade,
And saw that it was good.

So let us bear ourselves with pride
That we are part of such a place
A shining star in time and space,
Forever blessed by God's great grace,
To blossom in His love.

Margaret Ingall

Monday — **July 21**

I ALWAYS knew I wasn't the first person to notice that a smile helps the world go round, and I was amused to find that writer Joseph Addison had beaten me to it by more than three hundred years. He wrote:

"What sunshine is to flowers, smiles are to humanity. These are but trifles, to be sure; but scattered along life's pathway, the good they do is inconceivable."

And don't you think that idea alone is worth a smile?

Tuesday — **July 22**

WISDOM can be found in the most unusual circumstances. An unlikely candidate for anything athletic, our young friend Lee had jogged the length of his street and was planning, he told me as he stopped for a rest, on jogging back.

During his brief rest he laughed self-deprecatingly and said the words we can surely apply to almost every venture in life: "You don't have to be great to start, but you have to start to be great!"

Wednesday — **July 23**

BERNARD FONTENELLE was a lawyer in eighteenth-century France before becoming a novelist, so he knew a thing or two about the truth and how it should be used. "If I had my hand full of truth," he wrote, "I would take good care how I opened it!"

This reminded me of the advice given by a Quaker father to his son. "See thou be telling the truth – but see thou be not always telling it!"

Surely the last word on speaking truthfully has to go to the poet Kahlil Gibran who observed: "If indeed you must be candid, be candid beautifully!"

Thursday — **July 24**

YOU might think the Swiss philosopher and poet Henri Frederic Amiel a depressing sort of fellow when he observed: "Life is short!"

But there was good reason for his urgency. "We have not too much time," he went on, "to gladden the hearts of those who are travelling with us. Oh, be swift to love! Make haste to be kind!"

If we lived for a thousand years, we still would not have too much time for such an important mission.

Friday — **July 25**

YOU can tell a lot about people by the songs they sing. And this is why I was delighted to hear that the Porgy and Bess song "Summertime" has been translated into every known language in the world.

It's about family, about growing into your own person, and about that feeling of abundant life you can't escape in the midst of a really good summer.

I'd say that reflects rather well on us as people, wouldn't you?

Saturday — **July 26**

"WHAT are we celebrating, Gran?" the young lad asked. His grandmother laughed and said it was easy to think of something because at her age, she had learned how precious life is and would often say in conversation: "Every day is a bonus."

"Today," she said to Henry, "we are simply celebrating being together. We're enjoying ourselves, come sun or rain, having somewhere to go and something to talk about."

Henry seemed satisfied with this explanation. From that day on, he would always look forward to seeing his grandmother and the next celebration they shared together, whatever that turned out to be.

Sunday — **July 27**

HAPPY Sunday! But why, you may be asking. Is this day a special one? Well, of course it is and, if you don't believe me, try reading Zephaniah 3:17:

"The Lord your God is in your midst, a mighty one who will save; he will rejoice over you with gladness: he will quiet you by his love; he will exult over you with loud singing."

That sounds very special to me!

Monday — **July 28**

BETTY is a quiet friend of ours who devotes most of her time to looking after her family and her elderly mother and doesn't have much time to socialise and enjoy herself.

I am reminded of her because I read these words by Nathaniel Hawthorne, the author of "The Scarlet Letter": "Every individual has a place to fill in the world, and is important, in some respect, whether he chooses to be or not."

Betty would never think of herself as important. But, Mr Hawthorne was right. She is!

Tuesday — **July 29**

ON our old friend Mary's morning stroll, she passed the local school which was closed for the summer holidays. All of a sudden, a movement beneath the trees caught her attention and she stopped.

A squirrel suddenly scurried across the grass, and then a moment later a second one appeared. They had an energetic and playful game racing to and fro and were quite unaware of anyone being there. She was sorry when they scurried back amongst the trees and disappeared from view.

As our friend continued on her way, she smiled to herself as she wondered if the school children were enjoying their holiday half as much as these squirrels seemed to be!

Wednesday — **July 30**

ALL of us have occasionally lost our temper and said things in the heat of the moment which we regret later. In this context I'd like to offer this advice from the thirteenth-century Persian poet Rumi:

Raise your words, not your voice,
It is rain which grows flowers, not thunder.

Thursday — **July 31**

IT had been a grey and cloudy day. The Lady of the House and I had given up on the sun as evening approached but, suddenly, there was a completely unexpected break in the clouds and we hurried to the window for a better view.

Immediately our spirits lifted and though it was just a small amount of brightness, it seemed to offer hope and joy. The words of St Francis of Assisi, who was always so close to nature, came to mind: "A single sunbeam will drive away many shadows."

How right he was. I hope that when your life and your skies are overcast, you will always find at least one sunbeam to cheer you and lift your spirits.

August

Friday — **August 1**

GRANT'S flower beds in full bloom are a sight to behold. Still, he looked at them one afternoon and shook his head, as if there was something he didn't understand. I asked what was puzzling him.

"What did those flowers do to deserve to be so beautiful?" he asked.

Well, it wasn't the kind of question that can be answered easily, but Grant soon supplied his own thoughts on the matter.

"Nothing. The beauty was in them from the beginning, Francis. All they had to do was let it out."

And that thought stayed with me all day. He was talking about flowers – wasn't he?

Saturday — **August 2**

BOB has had many ups and downs during his career. Every time he has come across obstacles and disappointments, he has managed to pick himself up and is soon on top again. I know it's not the whole story, but these verses, framed and hanging in his office, must have something to do with his path to success:

Keep going,
It's better than sitting aside
Dreaming and waiting
The turn of the tide.
In life's daily battle they only prevail
Who boldly go forward
And never say fail.

PAISLEY PATTERN

Sunday — **August 3**

THIS is a hymn our old friend Mary has always found inspiring, "Leaning On The Everlasting Arms", written by Elisha A. Hoffman, a minister's son, who was ordained in 1868 and wrote over two thousand gospel songs.

As a child, she said, this hymn conjured up a vivid image of our heavenly Father's enduring faithfulness that she has always found inspiring. Regardless of what the day ahead may bring, He is the master of each moment and the firm foundation upon which we can confidently stand.

O how sweet to walk in this pilgrim way,
Leaning on the everlasting arms;
O how bright the path grows from day to day,
Leaning on the everlasting arms.
Leaning, leaning, safe and secure from all alarms;
Leaning, leaning, leaning on the everlasting arms.

"There is none holy as the Lord: for there is none beside thee: neither is there any rock like our God."   (Samuel 1 2:2)

Monday — **August 4**

THE Lady of the House was delighted with the cards and gifts she received on her birthday. The cards had all been chosen with care and the words from friends and relatives were quite touching.

"You see how highly thought of you are," I told her encouragingly.

She was still unsure and felt she didn't deserve the praise, so I reminded her of this quotation by Lois L. Kaufman: "Plant a seed of friendship, reap a bouquet of happiness."

"You have planted many seeds over the last year," I said. "Now it's time for your bouquet."

A glow of happiness spread over her face and I knew she would be eager and willing to plant even more seeds in the months to come. I hope we will all be ready to do the same.

Tuesday — **August 5**

GOODNIGHT, LORD

*B*IRDS *call across the treetops*
And coax young ones to their nests,
A sweet vesper on the breeze.
Goodnight, Lord.
Tender blades of grass
Dream of being bent beneath the weight
Of shining dew,
And tired posies on the lawn
Give a perfumed sigh.
Goodnight, Lord.
Across the street,
Mothers call their children,
A dog barks.
Goodnight, Lord.
He, who never sleeps,
Lights the chandeliers
Of the moon,
Pours out the Milky Way
And wraps the sky in violet tissue,
Tying it with starry ribbons.
Goodnight, my child.

Rachel Wallace-Oberle

Wednesday — **August 6**

THE novelist and satirist Mark Twain wasn't shy about his own virtues and he once declared: "I have a higher and grander standard of principle than George Washington. He could not lie; I can, but I won't!"

It was tongue-in-cheek but, as always, Mr Twain was hinting at a deeper truth. Life isn't simply about what we can or can't do. It's about what we can do but don't, what we can't do but try to, and what we don't need to do, but do anyway.

Thursday — **August 7**

IT had been such a lovely summer's day that the Lady of the House and I spent most of it pottering outside, and even after downing our gardening tools, we were reluctant to return indoors. So instead we sat down on our comfortable old bench and quietly watched as the sun went down.

It was the American minister Jonathan Edwards who observed: "Surely there is something in the unruffled calm of nature that overawes our little anxieties and doubts; the sight of the deep-blue sky and the clustering stars above seems to impart a quiet to the mind."

May you, too, be blessed with the peace of such a perfect summer gift.

Friday — **August 8**

ON a ferry crossing to one of the Western Isles of Scotland a passenger was amazed to hear that the captain couldn't swim. Safely on the other side, he decided to tease the captain about it.

"You should be pleased I can't swim," the captain replied with a straight face. "It means I will try harder to make sure my passengers don't have to!"

There's nothing like investing a bit of yourself in your work to make sure you do the very best that you can.

Saturday — **August 9**

HOW many times have you heard someone described as a ray of sunshine? Hopefully you know lots of people like that – they do make such a difference to life.

But sometimes that general sunshine needs to be focused on to a specific purpose. That's when we get the kind of people the writer Maya Angelou described as "a rainbow in somebody's cloud."

AWAY FROM IT ALL

Sunday — **August 10**

WILLIAM CAREY dedicated his life to spreading the gospel in India, serving as a missionary there from 1793 until his death in 1834. He hoped to translate Scripture into as many Indian languages and dialects as possible and established a large print shop where translators worked, as well as typesetters, compositors, pressmen and writers.

One day while he was teaching in Calcutta, a fire started in the printing room. Despite all efforts, the building burned to the ground, destroying the library, type sets, large quantities of paper, dictionaries, deeds and account books. His entire life's work was gone.

When he surveyed the scene, he wept and said, "In one short evening the labours of years are consumed. How unsearchable are the ways of God ... The Lord has laid me low, that I may look more simply to him."

Little did William Carey know that the fire would bring his work to the attention of people everywhere. Volunteers and donations helped rebuild and expand the printing operation, eventually publishing the Bible in many languages and dialects.

"But we have this treasure in earthen vessels that the excellence of the power may be of God and not of us."
(Corinthians II 4:7)

Monday — **August 11**

IT'S strange, isn't it, how some people have the knack of turning the most ordinary of houses into the most cheerful of places to live. However cramped or lacking in comforts, there is always enough room for a visitor, enough tea in the pot to pour an extra cup, and enough goodwill to make an unexpected guest feel truly welcome.

I think Victor Hugo summed it up best when he said: "A house is built of logs and stone, of tiles and piers; a home is built of loving deeds that stand a thousand years."

And I'd rather live in a loving home than a palace any day!

Tuesday — **August 12**

NOVELIST John Updike won two Pulitzer prizes by writing about ordinary people. But his descriptions of those people and their situations were anything but ordinary. Explaining his flamboyant descriptive style, Updike said he was merely giving "the mundane its beautiful due".

It amazes me that we ever find anything in this intricate, thriving and wonderfully arranged world boring, but sometimes we do. Thankfully, we have people like Mr Updike to remind us to give the day – each and every ordinary day – its beautiful due.

Wednesday — **August 13**

"**B**E strong, and of good courage,
Fear not, nor yet dismay
For God, our Lord is with us
Wherever we may stray."
Those Bible words bring comfort,
And so believe. Take heart!
Through all life's separations,
From God we never part.

Margaret Ingall

Thursday — **August 14**

SOMEONE once worked out that you would have to shout for eight years, seven months and six days to produce enough sound energy to heat a cup of coffee. All that effort for so little good effect!

Next time you feel like shouting in an attempt to change something, it might be better to actually boil the kettle, then sit down with the other person over two hot cups of coffee and sort things out. Perhaps with biscuits.

If nothing else it would save eight years, seven months and six days of wasted noise.

Friday — **August 15**

GOOD news! We wait for the postman to bring it in the mail, we hope to hear it when the phone rings, we love to share it with friends and few things can brighten a day the way it can.

With a maturity that far exceeded the almost sixteen years she lived, Anne Frank wrote: "Everyone has inside them a piece of good news. The good news is you don't know how great you can be! How much you can love! What you can accomplish! And what your potential is!"

Saturday — **August 16**

OUR young friend Janice enjoys her Irish dancing lessons. It is fun to watch and you can't help but admire the hard work and dedication that goes into it, but the scoring system has always been a mystery to me.

At least that was until I heard a judge at a recent competition explain that they only mark the positives, they aren't allowed to penalise faults.

Now, wouldn't it be wonderful if in the "jig of life" we treated our fellow dancers in the same way and rewarded their positive aspects without highlighting the negative?

Sunday — **August 17**

ONE of the things I like best about Sundays is that it usually, however busy our week has been, gives us the chance to pause and get life back in proportion. And how about this thought to help you?

"Let nothing disturb thee; let nothing dismay thee; all things pass; God never changes. Patience attains all that it strives for. He who has God finds he lacks nothing: God alone suffices."

These words come from St Teresa of Avila. They are wise ones, well worth remembering every day of the week.

Monday — **August 18**

WHEN you feel your world is empty,
Your prayers have gone unheard,
Reach out across the silence
With just one precious word.
A word to bring fresh warmth and joy
Recapturing the past,
With happy thoughts of sunlit days
And love designed to last.

With memories of youth and Spring,
Of Summer's light and shade,
Of sharing beauty, hopes and dreams
These pictures never fade.
Through all the seasons of the year
From April to December,
Reach out for all the love you've known,
And, once again, remember.

Iris Hesselden.

Tuesday — **August 19**

LIFE can never be easy if you happen to be the ninth of ten children born into a poor family in Massachusetts in 1824. Aged only eleven, Lucy Larcom was already working in a mill in order to help family finances, and her hopes of making her mark on the world seemed small.

But Lucy was no ordinary girl and, never one to allow bleak conditions to dishearten her, was soon writing and publishing idealistic poems, hymns and songs. Eventually her talent was recognised, and she went on to become first a teacher, then a respected full-time writer of inspirational and biographical works.

"If the world seems cold to you, kindle fires to warm it," she once advised her readers. And if anyone lit the way, Lucy Larcom surely did.

Wednesday — **August 20**

SOME of Amanda's colleagues were complaining about their workload and wishing they could work elsewhere. But they all stopped to think when Amanda shared the wisdom of American author Robert Fulghum who observed:

"The grass is not, in fact, always greener on the other side of the fence. No, not at all. Fences have nothing to do with it. The grass is greenest where it is watered. When crossing over fences, carry water with you and tend the grass wherever you may be."

Well said, indeed.

Thursday — **August 21**

ARE you feeling alone? Or are you perhaps overwhelmed by fears for the future, both for yourself or for those you care for?

Take courage, for there is One who is with us every moment of the day, and whose word brings eternal comfort: "There is nothing love cannot face; there is no limit to its faith, its hope and endurance."

Assurance indeed that God walks beside every one of us, and always will.

Friday — **August 22**

A SPECIAL RECIPE

TAKE understanding, love and care;
   Add tact and patience, then with flair
Mix faith and trust, a tender smile,
These gifts that make life so worthwhile,
And weigh upon the scales of life,
The special joys of man and wife.
This recipe will then ensure
True happiness will long endure.
                    Elizabeth Gozney

Saturday — **August 23**

SIR EDMUND HILLARY, one of the first men to set foot on the summit of Everest, said, "You don't have to be a fantastic hero to do certain things. You can be just an ordinary chap – sufficiently motivated."

Thankfully, there are a lot of people out there who are "sufficiently motivated" to do a good job, set a good example, and help raise their families. I can't think of many things more heroic. And when their quiet, steady efforts come to fruition I am sure they feel every bit as on top of the world as Sir Edmund did!

Sunday — **August 24**

WHAT'S your favourite day of the week? Dennis is in no doubt about his. "I love Sundays," he told me. "It's the one day when I make a deliberate effort to switch off all the workaday business of life. At first it almost felt as if I was being selfish, but now I see it as a positive necessity."

As the American writer Joseph Campbell puts it: "We're so engaged in doing things to achieve purposes of outer value that we forget the inner value, the rapture that is associated with being alive, is what it's all about."

Now that's a Sunday thought that's worth carrying through the whole week.

Monday — **August 25**

ACTOR Jim Carrey once observed the following: "Flowers don't worry about how they're going to bloom. They just open up and turn toward the light, and that makes them beautiful."

Want to be beautiful? Don't worry about expensive cosmetics or a makeover, just follow Mr Carrey's advice. Find the light in your life that makes you bloom. Then open up and turn towards it!

Tuesday — **August 26**

OVERHEARD snatches of conversation remind me how many unsung philosophers there are amongst us. The woman in the supermarket queue was complaining that someone she knew only ever called when she needed something.

"Hmm …" her companion replied. Then a thought seemed to occur to her. "Do you think candles mind that we only reach for them when there's darkness in our lives?"

A candle in someone's darkness; even if we never see other aspects of their life, that's surely still worthwhile.

Wednesday — **August 27**

DO you recall reading the memorable words of this old rhyme?

Have you ever leant upon a gate, without a need for words,
To take in nature's wonder, and listen to the birds?
Yes, leaning on a gate is a thing we ought to do.
It helps us to unwind and such moments are so few.

The last few words take a beautiful notion, and then remind us that the opportunities to indulge in it are regrettably few.

I would agree – and also disagree. Gates to lean on are scarcer these days, and yet they still manage to appear to people who know how to make the best use of them.

Thursday — **August 28**

WOULDN'T it be wonderful to have a life without difficulties? Well, I'm sure it sounds a pleasing prospect but would it be worth the price?

What price, you may ask. Well, I'm thinking of Jean de la Bruyère who wrote: "Out of difficulties grow miracles."

If we learned to see the tricky times we all encounter less as problems and more as offering the potential for miracles, we might welcome a few more into our lives!

Friday — **August 29**

IF you ruled the world you would have everything you needed to be happy, or so you might think. Well, in the second century A.D. Marcus Aurelius very nearly did rule the world – after all, he was the Emperor of Rome!

But he was shrewd and said: "Very little is needed to make a happy life; it is all within yourself, in your way of thinking."

So, take a tip from one who knew. Go out today and be the ruler of your own empire of happiness!

Saturday — **August 30**

MAHATMA GHANDI had many thoughts about life well worth sharing. "The difference between what we do and what we are capable of doing," he once pointed out, "would suffice to solve most of the world's problems."

Now, you and I might not make much of an impact on the world's problems, but if we truly did all we were capable of we could make a marked difference to our own situation – and those of the people around us.

Sunday — **August 31**

IN his 1867 novel "Annals Of A Quiet Neighbourhood" George MacDonald presents himself as the new minister in an English village. Being only just appointed to the parish he doesn't know anyone. Then he meets Old Rogers and realises, "I had found a friend already – that is, a man to whom I might possibly be of some use."

I'm sure Rev. MacDonald would have agreed that a life of service among God's children is the best way of giving thanks to our Father. And, as he pointed out, it's an excellent way to make friends.

"Each of you should use whatever gift you have received to serve others, as faithful stewards of God's grace in its various forms."   (Peter 1 4:10)

September

Monday — **September 1**

SEPTEMBER is often a beautiful month, although summer is drawing to a close. Now, I know that some of us can feel a little sad at this prospect, with the ending of long, sunny summer days and many chilly, dark winter weeks to come. But autumn can be delightful, a rich season with its own delights, and I think this verse by nineteeth-century writer Helen Hunt Jackson sums it all up to perfection:

> *By all these lovely tokens*
> *September days are here,*
> *With summer's best of weather*
> *And autumn's best of cheer.*

So enjoy the September sunshine when you can and don't forget all the glories of autumn yet to come!

Tuesday — **September 2**

THERE used to be just alcoves where the bins sat. They were set in a roughcast wall; there was a path, a low brick wall and a main road. Not a very pretty sight.

Then a couple of the neighbours got together, arranged for wrought iron gates to be made for the alcoves, and installed large plant pots behind the metalwork. Now, through spring, summer and autumn, that grey stretch of wall is lit up with a blaze of brightly coloured flowers, which I'm sure uplift the spirits of many of those driving by as well as residents.

Is there any dreary corner of our lives that can't be made to shine a little brighter? See if you can start to shed a new light on something mundane today.

Wednesday — **September 3**

AT ninety years of age George Dawson discovered a new way to express himself. He learned to read and write!

The former road repairer, dairyman and saw mill worker, who had helped all his children with their homework, despite never understanding a written word or ever putting pencil to paper, then went on to write a book. It was published when he was 103!

And what did he call it? "Life Is So Good!"

Having discovered a brand-new way to communicate with the world, I don't think Mr Dawson could have picked a better subject – or a more apt title.

Thursday — **September 4**

MANY LESSONS TO LEARN

So many people teach us as we travel through each day,
So many people lead us, guide us back when we're astray,
From nursery to schooldays; at work and in our play
We learn from those around us as they help us on our way.
Yet let us not forget, of course, we too can play our part,
We too can be wise teachers, there's no secret to the art,
We simply have to live our life with kind and loving heart,
For that's the finest lesson that we ever could impart.

Margaret Ingall

Friday — **September 5**

EDUCATIONALIST Janet Erskine Stuart believed in the potential of her pupils, and one of her maxims might just as easily apply to those of us a little older than school age.

Writing before the First World War she observed: "To aim at the best and to remain essentially ourselves is one and the same thing."

We each have "the best" at the heart of us.

SAFE STRONGHOLD

Saturday — **September 6**

DOING NOTHING

DO nothing every now and then,
It helps you to relax,
And let your thoughts go wandering
Along some mountain tracks.
Do nothing – it's quite wonderful,
Watch raindrops on the glass,
See the leaves float in the autumn,
Sunbeams on the grass.

See the way the clouds keep moving
High above the trees,
Find a little peace and quiet,
Moments sure to please.
If your batteries need recharging
And life has lost its smile,
Be still, and let the world go by,
Do nothing for a while.

Iris Hesselden.

Sunday — **September 7**

WE are often encouraged to count our blessings, and if we do we usually find we can't count high enough. We might want to give a little back for all we have received, but what can we possibly offer to the God who created everything?

Well, the great writer, inventor, publisher and diplomat Benjamin Franklin gave the matter some thought and came up with this beautiful answer: "O powerful Goodness! Bountiful Father! Merciful Guide! ... Accept my kind offices to Thy other children as the only return in my power for Thy continual favours to me."

"Dear friends, since God so loved us, we also ought to love one another." (John 1 4:11)

Monday — **September 8**

THE German author Erich Maria Remarque met an American woman in Berlin. When she asked him why he had never visited the United States, he explained that he only knew a few phrases in English.

She asked what they were and he replied, "How do you do? I love you. Forgive me. And, ham and eggs please."

"Sakes alive," she replied, "with that vocabulary you could tour my country from Maine to California!"

An extensive vocabulary is a good thing but we could steer our way pleasantly through this life with a surprisingly small selection of words. Find the good ones – and use them!

Tuesday — **September 9**

GOOD days are not hard to find – but a perfect day? What would be involved in making one of those?

A wise lady called Ruth Smeltzer offered this suggestion: "You have not lived a perfect day, unless you have done something for someone who will never be able to repay you."

Wednesday — **September 10**

SPOCK, the half-Vulcan, half-human character in the television series "Star Trek" would greet people with a raised hand (fingers split in a "V" formation) and the words: "Live long and prosper."

Well, I'm sure we'll all live as long as we can but when it comes to prospering it might have been helpful if Spock had explained how. Thankfully, Leonard Nimoy, the actor who played Spock, had the answer.

"The miracle is this," he said. "The more we share the more we have."

Perhaps our Vulcan friend should have said: "Live long and share ... and prosper."

Thursday — **September 11**

I OFTEN meet Alan when I am out and about and it's always a pleasure to do so. You see, Alan has what I consider to be one of the best good mornings ever. Let me explain.

"Good morning!" might be all he says, but he pronounces these two words in such a memorable and meaningful way.

Then I met his wife one morning and she said "Good morning!" in exactly the same way.

It occurred to me that each might have subconsciously copied the other over the years. Many of us are quick to find fault with those in our closest circle, but wouldn't it make for a more enriched life if, instead of picking fault, we chose the best attributes and then made more of them?

Friday — **September 12**

" PATIENCE and perseverance have a magical effect before which difficulties disappear and obstacles vanish."

John Quincy Adams

Saturday — **September 13**

I F you find yourself in the Ashmolean Museum in Oxford you might spend a pleasant few minutes looking at their posie rings. These are gold rings, some dating from the fifteenth century with rhymes inscribed around them. They were used as wedding rings or gifts to friends and some of the sentiments will raise a smile while others will touch the heart:

As God decreed so we agreed:
I cannot show the love I owe:
Of earthly joys thou art my choice:
Here is my heart – guard it well.

The tradition isn't as popular these days but it might be worth considering which words you would commit to gold – and then give away.

Sunday — **September 14**

I T'S Harvest Festival time again! But do you know that the festival as we celebrate it today was "invented" as recently as the mid-1840s? Although part of the church calendar since medieval times, it had gradually been forgotten until Robert Stephen Hawker, the vicar of Morwentstow in Cornwall, decided to change things.

To call Rev. Hawker an eccentric would almost be an understatement, for his behaviour was as colourful as his very non-clerical clothes. He talked to birds, excommunicated his cat for mousing on Sundays, and kept a large pig as a pet.

He was, however, also greatly loved by his parishioners so when on 1st October, 1843 he invited them to a new kind of harvest festival, they were happy to approve his efforts, which had included decking the church from top to toe with vegetables, flowers, fruit and bread. Indeed so popular was Rev. Hawker's version of Harvest Festival that it soon became accepted everywhere.

Today it remains one of our favourite festivals – and this time when we join in the praise, let us give thanks not just for the harvest, but for the work of Robert Stephen Hawker, whose joy of living enriched so many lives.

Monday — **September 15**

P ERHAPS the questioner was being flippant, or perhaps he thought he'd catch the wise man out.

"Tell me why people raise their voices to each other when they are angry," he said. "After all, they are usually face to face and can hear each other perfectly well."

The wise man thought about it, as wise men do, and said, "It is because they are not talking face to face, they are trying to talk heart to heart, and their hearts are so far apart when they are angry."

The questioner wasn't convinced. So, the wise man added, "That's why lovers whisper to each other."

Tuesday — **September 16**

"THERE are only three colours," someone once said to our old friend Mary. The words came back to her one day as she was wandering round a London art gallery, lost in admiration of what painters had been able to achieve with the primary colours, blue, green and red.

Of course the skill is in how they mix them and how they are applied.

We might have a limited range of opportunities available to us as we go through life. But with imagination and dedication we can mix and apply them in the best possible way, eventually painting a picture of our lives the Old Masters would envy!

Wednesday — **September 17**

I'D LIKE to share these thought-provoking words by Oliver Wendell Holmes with you today:

Where we love is home,
Home that our feet may leave,
But not our hearts.

Thursday — **September 18**

ANDREW Carnegie was born in a humble cottage in Dunfermline in 1835. He deserves to be remembered, not for the vast fortune he made, but for giving so much of it to deserving causes.

He emigrated with his parents to the United States, and through hard work and business acumen, became one of that country's biggest figures on the industrial scene. His fortune secure, he began donating sums, large and small, to charities of all kinds. There are still many public libraries in the UK that were founded by him.

Andrew Carnegie set an example of giving that continues to be followed by leading entrepreneurs of today.

Friday — **September 19**

HIDDEN camera television shows aim to provide laughs by putting people into unexpected situations. But when the original "Candid Camera" programme was aired, its producers had a different approach. Their philosophy was: "We believe people are wonderful, and we're out to confirm it."

It's an idea I find proof of every day – and I'm being completely candid about that!

Saturday — **September 20**

GOODBYE

SUMMER dances down the lane
In robes of golden light,
With sunshine streaming from her face
All dazzling clear and bright.

She brings with her the butterflies,
The ghostly moths at dusk,
And heady scents of honeysuckle,
Jasmine, rose and musk.

Foxgloves, stocks and hollyhocks,
Delphiniums, sweet peas,
Extend an invitation to
The busy honey bees.

But all too soon she has to go
She's sung her summer song,
The season's coming to its end
And she has stayed too long.

Passing by on nimble feet
She turns to catch my eye,
Reluctantly I raise my hand
To wave a fond goodbye.

                    Kathleen Gillum

Sunday — **September 21**

CAN you imagine saying a prayer before eating an apple? Well, the Hebrew book of prayer has a prayer specifically for tasting the first fruit of the season:

"Blessed art thou, O Lord our God, King of the universe, who hast kept us in life, and hast preserved us, and hast enabled us to reach this season."

The season referred to might be when fruit ripens, when something we have been waiting for comes to completion, the time of year or a season in our life. With a little appreciation and thanks they might all taste as sweet as that first fruit.

"There is a time for everything, and a season for every activity under the heavens." (Ecclesiastes 3:1)

Monday — **September 22**

IT was sunny and warm after a week of cloud and rain. The Lady of the House immediately decided it was a day for being out and about. She picked up an anthology of favourite poems and quotations and said: "We are not the only ones to feel like this."

I was reminded of these words by Richard Le Gallienne:

I meant to do my work today,
But a brown bird sang in the apple tree,
And a butterfly flitted across the field,
And all the leaves were calling me.
And the wind went sighing over the land
Tossing the grasses to and fro,
And a rainbow held out its shining hand
So what could I do but laugh and go?

What indeed! Together we enjoyed the sunshine and the people we encountered looked cheerful and smiling. Returning home, we gave thanks for the gifts of nature and the joy of sunshine.

NEARLY THERE!

Tuesday — **September 23**

ONCE upon a time cowboys dominated the silver screen. If you turned on the television or went to the cinema you were almost guaranteed to find Roy Rogers, the Lone Ranger or Hopalong Cassidy putting the world to rights.

Decency, humour and truth were qualities these Hollywood heroes held dear – in fact, Roy Rogers even had his own prayer which reflected that humble faith:

Lord, I reckon I'm not much just by myself,
I fail at a lot of things I ought to do.
But, Lord, when trails are steep and passes high,
Help me ride it straight the whole way through.
And when, in the falling dusk, I get that final call,
I do not care how many flowers they send.
Above all else the happiest trail would be
For you to say to me, "Let's ride, my friend."

Wednesday — **September 24**

HOW irritating it is to find a roll of parcel tape with the end stuck down, almost invisible. It makes you long for a good old-fashioned ball of string to tie up your parcels.

The Lady of the House never uses scissors to cut string off a parcel, and always stores it away to use again. I tipped out her string bag one wet winter's morning and looked at the tangled mass – lots of soft white string, mixed with brown twine and chunky sisal, all jumbled together.

"Just like us," I thought. "Sometimes we're all mixed up!" With a little patience I began to untangle all the string, and then rolled it up neatly again ready to be re-used. It reminded me of the hymn that says, "… my heart was free!"

I can be patient when untying a bag of string and I try to show the same patience towards others who are entwined with worries, tangled up in their anxieties. Truly, there is nothing like a kind word to unravel the knots inside, so let's try to ease someone's mind today.

Thursday — **September 25**

THEY say the best things in life are free. We might only discover the importance of this when we're older, having pursued things that have had little lasting value.

We all have many simple but enriching blessings around us, if we take time to think about them, and as we consider them, our sense of contentment will surely increase and we'll appreciate those gifts more, no matter how small they might appear to be at first glance.

So if you are having a difficult day, take a moment to count a few of your blessings. You'll soon feel better. And it will have cost you nothing!

Friday — **September 26**

HAVE your heard of Johann Olav Koss? You may well have done, for as an Olympic skater he has broken eleven world records and holds four gold medals. However, it's for something that was almost a mistake, of which he is perhaps most proud. Let me explain.

As a young ambassador for Olympic Aid visiting the starving population of Eritrea, he impulsively arranged for the youngsters of Norway to send thousands of soccer balls to their peers in Africa.

It wasn't until the balls actually arrived that he realised a population desperately short of food might be less than impressed by a donation of sports equipment.

But President Isaias Afewerki was able to reassure him. "This is the most beautiful gift we have ever received," he said. "Finally we are being seen as human beings. We are more than mouths to feed. We are people – we, too, have dreams and we hope for a better future."

Today Johann Olav Koss is honorary chairman of Right To Play, a charity dedicated to providing, via sports, a pathway to all kinds of health and education projects. Isn't it good to think that a soccer ball can score such a world-changing goal?

Saturday — **September 27**

OUR old friend Mary has an old prayer card that belonged to her grandmother and each night she reads these words by Samuel Bagster:

> *The Lord Bless thee —*
> *How shall he bless thee?*
> *With the gladness that knoweth no decay*
> *With the riches that cannot pass away*
> *With the sunshine that makes an endless day —*
> *Thus may he bless thee.*
> *And keep thee —*
> *How shall he keep thee?*
> *With the all-covering shadow of his wings*
> *And the strong love that guards from evil things*
> *With the sure power that safe to glory brings —*
> *Thus may he keep thee.*

As a child, Samuel Bagster (1772-1851) was brought up a devoted Christian, a faith that sustained him throughout his life. This highly-principled religious bookshop owner would gather his family together daily for reading God's Word, linking the day's verses with other Bible passages, and praying about how it could be applied. His "Daily Light" is one of the most loved devotionals of all time.

Sunday — **September 28**

JACK NICKLAUS was once being interviewed by a really gushy reporter. Singing his praises, the reporter then said, "You really know your way around a golf course! What's the secret?"

Nicklaus replied, "The holes are numbered!"

The "secrets" behind great things are often simple. Like the secret behind living a life of faith:

"He has shown you, O mortal, what is good. And what does the Lord require of you? To act justly and to love mercy and to walk humbly with your God."   (Micah 6:8)

Monday — **September 29**

AS TIME GOES BY

WHEN the years flash by
In the blink of an eye,
No sooner the start than the end.
When the bells of Time
Have a hollow chime,
And bits of you creak when you bend.
When that wavy hair
Is no longer there
And nothing hangs quite where it should,
And the spirit is willing
For all that is thrilling,
And, oh, but you would, if you could.

Well, don't lose hope
On that downward slope.
Relax, and enjoy the view.
Let the edifice crumble
As pipes groan and grumble,
That's just the façade, never you.
Life's swift little feet
Can never defeat
That secret, quite hid and unseen,
Which no-one can know,
But undoubtedly so . . .
Deep inside, you are still seventeen!

Tricia Sturgeon

Tuesday — **September 30**

HERE are two thoughts to bear in mind as you go through today or indeed any day of the week:

Smile – it increases your face value.
Smile – sunshine is good for your teeth.

October

Wednesday — **October 1**

AMY, aged six, wrote a letter which read: "Dear God, how did you get invented?" Her father sent a copy of her letter to the Archbishop of Canterbury, Rowan Williams, who wrote back to the young girl saying, "I think God might reply a bit like this:

"Nobody invents me – but lots of people discovered me and were quite surprised. They discovered me when they looked round the world and thought it was really beautiful or really mysterious and wondered where it came from. They discovered me when they were very quiet on their own and felt a sort of peace and love they hadn't expected."

I think we can all learn from this letter.

Thursday — **October 2**

POSITIVE-NEGATIVE

IF we should look for faults and flaws
We'll find them, that's for sure.
If gloom and grumbles be our goal
We'll own them by the score.
Yet strange to say, that in reverse,
The same is always found.
If we should seek out blessings, well –
Just look – they're all around!
I know which I would rather find:
It's things to make me smile.
It's positives, not negatives,
That make our lives worthwhile.

Margaret Ingall

Friday — **October 3**

LIFE should be a process of continuous learning. If you let a dog be your teacher, you would learn such things as these:

When loved ones come home, rush to greet them.
Don't pass up the chance to go for an outing in the car and let the experience of fresh air and the wind in your face feel great.
Thrive on attention and let people touch you.
On warm days, take time to lie down on the grass.
On hot days, drink lots of water and lie in the shade.
Delight in the simple joy of a long walk.
Be loyal.
If you desire what lies buried, dig until you find it.
If someone is having a bad day, sit quietly nearby, and nuzzle them gently.

Yes, we can learn many valuable lessons from our canine friends.

Saturday — **October 4**

SEVERAL years ago there was a story in the San Francisco Chronicle about a female humpback whale which had become entangled in crab traps and lines.

A fisherman spotted her struggling to stay afloat and called an environmental group for help. When the rescue team arrived, they decided the only way to save her was to dive in and untangle her. It was a dangerous venture – just one slap of her tail could kill a rescuer.

The team worked for hours and eventually freed her. When she was free, the divers said she swam in joyous circles. And then she came back to each diver, one at a time, and nudged them gently, as if thanking them. They said it was the most incredibly beautiful experience of their lives.

"If the only prayer you said in your whole life was 'Thank you,' that would suffice."   Meister Eckhart

Sunday — **October 5**

HELEN Keller is known around the world as a symbol of courage in the face of overwhelming odds. She was a woman of great intelligence, ambition and accomplishment, who dedicated her life to advocacy and activism that opened the doors of possibility for people with disabilities.

Born in 1880 in Alabama, Helen contracted an illness when nineteen months old that left her deaf and blind. But despite all the odds, with the help of Ann Sullivan, Helen learned to communicate and went on to become a world-famous speaker and author. In 1915 she founded Helen Keller International, an organisation devoted to research in vision, health and nutrition.

Helen said, "I thank God for my handicaps for through them, I have found myself, my work and my God."

"The spirit of God hath made me, and the breath of the Almighty hath given me life." (Job 33:4)

Monday — **October 6**

SPRING can be beautiful when all the brightly-coloured blossoms and blooms begin to appear. Surely autumn, when they all start to fade away, must be a sadder season?

Not according to French writer and philosopher Albert Camus. He chose to look up from the withered beds and borders to the blazing trees and said, "Autumn is a second spring where every leaf is a flower."

Tuesday — **October 7**

DESIGNER Ralph Lauren once said, "We all get report cards in many different ways, but the real excitement of what you're doing is in the doing of it. It's not what you're going to get in the end. It's not the final curtain. It's really in the doing it and loving what you're doing."

Now, that's how to design a life!

GOLDEN MOMENT

Wednesday — **October 8**

IT was a cartoon sketch that made the Lady of the House smile on a wet and windy day. It showed a stone and a twelve-inch ruler with big smiles on their "faces." The stone was pointing at its wooden friend and saying: "You rule!" The strip of wood was returning the favour, saying: "You rock!"

A fine example of what I've always believed, that no-one isn't improved by a little appreciation and, once you get to know them, there isn't anyone (or anything) that doesn't have something about them worth appreciating.

Thursday — **October 9**

HERE are a few inspiring quotes to take with you into the day:

"Always be a first-rate version of yourself instead of a second-rate version of somebody else."   Judy Garland

"Live in each season as it passes; breathe the air, drink the drink, taste the fruit, and resign yourself to the influences of each."   Henry David Thoreau

Friday — **October 10**

YOU know, of all the wonders and achievements of modern life, I still think that books, and our easy access to them, is the most impressive.

Just think – books are so commonplace, yet they can open all sorts of doors. They can put us in touch with distant civilisations, forge bonds with people we've never met, and help us to understand not just others, but ourselves as well.

And I'd include works of fiction in that. As writer Ben Okri put it: "Stories can conquer fear, you know. They can make the heart bigger."

And if that isn't a wonder, then I don't know what is.

Saturday — **October 11**

A MAN was selling helium-filled balloons at a fairground. Whenever business was slow he would release a brightly-coloured balloon. Children would see it fly up into the sky and look around, wondering where it came from. Then they might ask their parents to buy them one.

Having seen a red, orange and pink balloon fly skywards, one little lad plucked up the courage to ask if the dark blue one would do the same. Being assured it would, he asked: "Well, what about a star-shaped one?"

The balloon seller replied: "It doesn't matter what colour or shape the balloon is. It's what's inside it that makes it rise!"

He might have added that it's the same with people. It's not how we look but what's inside that makes us rise.

Sunday — **October 12**

TALKING TO GOD

D EAR Father, hear the prayer I pray,
You've heard it many times,
But knowing I can talk to You
My weary spirit climbs.
I ask for healing every day
For all the aches and pains,
And You send comfort, help and strength
As hope and love remains.

Dear Father, help the ones I love,
I know You understand,
Be with them in the storms of life
And take them by the hand.
Now thank you for the gifts of life,
I count them as before,
Tomorrow, Father, I'll be here
And talk to You once more.
Iris Hesselden

Monday — **October 13**

I KNOW it's not uncommon to see a sign over an establishment advertising a change of management, but I had to look twice when I saw a large banner above a doorway proclaiming a *Change of Attitude*.

However, that sign didn't just make me smile, it also made me think about the words I'd seen. They reminded me how important a change of attitude can be.

You see, even when we don't have the power to change the world around us, we do at least have the ability to adjust the way we think about things. It's surprising how much this can help, which is why I reckon it's worth a try – well, that's the way I'm choosing to think about it!

Tuesday — **October 14**

THE race is to the swiftest, so often we are told,
And those who don't move quickly will never gain the gold.
But who says winning prizes should be our only aim?
If that's our single object, then life's a sorry game.
So stop and look around you; don't always rush along,
Drink in this world of beauty; pay heed to Earth's great song.

M.J. Brison

Wednesday — **October 15**

MHAIRI looked at the falling leaves, and sighed. "You know," she observed, "as much as I love the beautiful autumn colours, I always experience sadness to think that another year is almost over."

Then she smiled. "But on the other hand, if I didn't feel sad now, then I don't suppose I'd be so thrilled when spring comes round again."

I recall reading these words which seem particularly apt: "Everything that has a beginning has an ending. Make your peace with that and all will be well."

Thursday — **October 16**

" **I** DON'T know how I managed to bite my tongue, but it's a good job I did, because it turned out she really hadn't meant what I thought she had …" The snippet of conversation floated to me across the street, and even though I couldn't identify the speaker, I silently congratulated her.

It's so easy to blurt out a hasty remark which, whether or not it's deserved, hardly ever improves a situation, and will often make it worse. Or, as an old motoring friend of mine used to say: "Always engage brain before putting mouth in gear!"

Friday — **October 17**

DO you ever think that the world seems to be becoming a more self-centred place at times? If we believe all we see and read, it would at times be easy to believe so.

However, what we shouldn't forget is that while stories of greed and self-interest tend to make the news headlines, they are vastly outnumbered by the instances of uncelebrated acts of unselfishness, which are carried out almost unthinkingly everywhere.

And if you're still not convinced, think about these words of Brother James Kimpton: "Much of what we do is like planting trees under which we may never sit, but plant we must."

Enjoy that dappled shade!

Saturday — **October 18**

IT IS my greatest pleasure to share with you all kinds of words of wisdom from all kinds of people. But while Aldous Huxley is a well-known name, I had to smile at his almost-apology for his supposed lack of profundity:

"It's a bit embarrassing to have been concerned with the human problem all one's life and find at the end that one has no more to offer by way of advice than try to be a little kinder."

But I can't think of anything wiser, can you?

Sunday — **October 19**

A MEDITATION

*O*UR *Father in heaven, hallowed be your Name,*
Bless all your children.
*Your Kingdom come, your will be done on earth
    as it is in heaven . . .*
Bless all the countries in the world. Give them
    peace and good government.

Give us this day our daily bread,
Feed the hungry, the starving, those out of work,
    all poor nations.

*Forgive us our sins as we forgive those who sin
    against us,*
Bless those we have hurt in body, mind or spirit
    knowingly or unknowingly. Help us to make
    good the harm we have done.

*Lead us not into temptation but deliver us
    from evil,*
Do not let the love of things separate us from
    the love of God.

*For the kingdom, the power and the glory are
    yours now and forever,*
May the world be filled with your Goodness and
    Glory as the waters cover the sea.

Amen. So be it.

Monday — **October 20**

EXTRAORDINARY things can be done in ordinary situations with the most ordinary of materials. It's all about how you use them.

Novelist Hamilton Wright Mabie wrote: "The question for each man (or woman) is not what he would do if he had the means, time, influence and educational advantages, but what he will do with the things he has."

Tuesday — **October 21**

OUR old friend Mary discovered this prayer written by Ralph Waldo Emerson. Think about these words today:

Write it on your heart
That every day is the best day in the year.
He is rich who owns the day, and no one owns the day
Who allows it to be invaded with fret and anxiety.

Finish every day and be done with it.
You have done what you could.
Some blunders and absurdities no doubt crept in.

Forget them as soon as you can, tomorrow is a new day;
Begin it well and serenely, with too high a spirit
To be cumbered with your old nonsense.

This new day is too dear,
With its hopes and invitations,
To waste a moment on the yesterdays.

Wednesday — **October 22**

A.A. MILNE'S delightful Winnie the Pooh has delighted many generations of children – and adults, too! So many times he makes the wisest remarks. For example, these words from "Pooh's Most Grand Adventure" really appeal to me.

As always, Christopher Robin and Pooh were spending time together in the Hundred Acre Wood. Pooh says to Christopher Robin: "You are just in time for the best part of the day."

Christopher Robin asks: "What part is that?" and Pooh replies: "The part where 'you and me' become 'we'!"

This made me think how we should all be grateful for the time we spend with friends and loved ones. These moments are so precious, yet pass by so quickly.

So the next time you meet up with someone close to you, remember Winnie the Pooh and how wonderful it is when "you and me" become "we"!

Thursday — **October 23**

"THANK goodness I didn't take it personally," Joanne said. "I've seen my neighbour three or four times this week, and she's virtually ignored me. I was beginning to feel upset until she suddenly confided that she'd been extremely worried about her sister who had been in a bad accident."

It's easy to assume that if something's going wrong then it must be to do with us. I don't know who first said it, but I do agree with the advice that we should always "be kinder than necessary because everyone you meet is fighting some kind of battle."

And even if we cannot provide help, at least we can be understanding and lend a listening ear.

Friday — **October 24**

IT'S said that children laugh or smile around four hundred times a day, while adults laugh or smile a mere twenty-five times a day. The Bible tells us we should become like little children to enter the Kingdom of Heaven. If we only relearned the habit of smiling and laughing more often, we might bring a little more Heaven into our days here on Earth.

Saturday — **October 25**

IF you feel you are being held back in life, perhaps it is because of that invisible element – fear. Fear holds us in our own little comfort zone, preventing us from taking any risks.

However, if we shun that comfort zone and tackle the things that we are a little afraid of, we become more liberated and claim back some strength for ourselves. And who knows, perhaps those dreams which we've been too fearful of pursuing will materialise. The highest risk in life is surely to take no risks at all.

So try to overcome your trepidation and take a small risk today – see how good a new step forward makes you feel.

THE FALL

Sunday — **October 26**

JANIE was recalling the old Sunday School song "The Wise Man Built His House Upon The Rock." When her husband Tom joined in with some of the hand actions she stopped, surprised.

"I went to Sunday School too, you know," he said, smiling.

"Yes, but you always tell me the only thing you remembered was your inspirational teacher."

Tom admitted he was surprised he remembered the song so clearly. He didn't remember any of the other teachers well or the activities he had taken part in. But what he did remember so well was the influence of one person.

That's surely what the essence of faith is. It's not about the songs, or the studies; it's about the effect it has on your life, the man or woman you become because of it.

And wise men and women show others, like Tom, how to build their homes upon "the Rock."

Monday — **October 27**

"SHARING! It's not what it's cracked up to be," Maureen grumbled one day.

Now I know very few folk who are more generous than our friend Maureen. In fact, I don't know anyone more giving of her time, help and encouragement. It wasn't like her to be speaking ill of a quality like sharing so the Lady of the House just had to ask for an explanation.

"I was so happy yesterday," explained Maureen. "To be honest, I had more happiness than I could handle. So I thought I would share it out – you know, give some to folk who didn't have as much as me."

She shook her head. "It didn't work, you know."

With a sigh that didn't quite hide the beginnings of a smile she said, "I ended up with even more of the blessed stuff!"

Tuesday — **October 28**

OUR friends Linda and Dave had been leaning on a five-bar gate watching dawn light turn into the morning sky. "The brevity of it makes it all the more beautiful," Dave observed.

"Yes," Linda replied. "The sun's always setting or rising somewhere."

The thought stayed with her until she arrived home and looked up a few lines by the Scots-born naturalist John Muir:

"The grand show is eternal. It is always sunrise somewhere; the dew is never dried all at once; a shower is forever falling; vapour is ever rising. Eternal sunrise, eternal dawn and gloaming, on sea and continents and islands, each in its turn, as the round earth rolls."

It seems there is nothing brief about nature's glory!

Wednesday — **October 29**

THERE is a proverb that says: "The best time to plant a tree was 20 years ago. The next best time is now." Wangari Maathai believed that the planting of trees is the planting of ideas and that when we dig a hole and plant a tree, we plant hope not only for ourselves but also for future generations.

A visionary, human rights advocate and environmental activist, Wangari founded the Green Belt Movement in Kenya. This unique organisation has planted over thirty-five million trees and now works internationally to empower communities to protect the environment and promote good governance and peace worldwide.

Wangari's powerful legacy includes being the first African woman to receive the Nobel Peace Prize. Her unforgettable words are a challenge to all to make this world a better place:

"There comes a time when humanity is called to shift to a new level of consciousness, to reach a higher moral ground. A time when we have to shed our fear and give hope to each other. That time is now."

A SONG FOR EVERYMAN

THERE is music in the mountains
And there's rhythm in the rain,
There is music in the treetops
And the blackbird's sweet refrain.

There is harmony in swaying grass
As it whispers by the lake,
And melody in morning wind
As it stirs the day awake.

There is whistling by the paper boy
As he hurries on his way,
And singing in the village church
To celebrate the day.

There is music deep within each heart
If we but seek and find,
And the music of the universe
Can soothe a troubled mind.

There is music all around us,
A song since time began,
A melody of joy and hope,
A song for everyman.

Iris Hesselden

Friday — **October 31**

IN the 1960s J. Paul Getty had more money that anyone else in the world. His brother, who didn't have a fraction of his money, but did have a loving family, once sent him a letter addressed like this: "To the wealthiest man in the world, from the richest man in the world."

It's a wise person who can tell the difference!

November

Saturday — **November 1**

IT had been a busy week for Harry with little time to himself, so he decided to take time out for a walk one evening to find a little peace and quiet. He walked along the rural tranquillity of the village canal bank. The evening was peaceful and far from the non-stop pace of daily life – only the ducks on the water and the birds in the trees could be heard.

Later, as the sun was setting, Harry found an old bench and sat there for a little while. As the peace flowed into his heart and mind, he recalled a hymn by John Greenleaf Whittier:

> *Drop thy still dews of quietness*
> *Till all our strivings cease,*
> *Take from our lives the strain and stress*
> *And let our ordered lives confess*
> *The beauty of thy peace.*

As Harry returned home in the dusk, he thought what a wonderful gift a little quietness can be, and how much we all need it.

Sunday — **November 2**

HOW do you please God? Aurelius Ambrosius, an English saint, said it was simple. "The grace of the Lord is won with a good life," he observed.

Many of us try to live good lives and fall short of our own expectations. But, like any loving father, God appreciates our efforts. He is, surely, pleased anew each time we try again.

"As for other matters, brothers and sisters, we instructed you how to live in order to please God, as in fact you are living. Now we ask you and urge you in the Lord Jesus to do this more and more." (Thessalonians I 4:1)

Monday — **November 3**

A PRAYER FOR WINTER

THE winter seems a long time, Lord,
A long time until spring,
A long time 'til we see green shoots
And hear the small birds sing.
So whilst the days are short and dark
Please keep us safe and strong,
Let cheerful music lift our souls,
Place in our hearts a song.

Through wintry winds, through frost and fog,
Let every doubt dispel,
And let your love fill all our lives
And whisper "all is well."
We thank you, Lord, for home and food,
The blessings of each day,
Let hope and joy light up our world
'Til winter slips away.

Iris Hesselden

Tuesday — **November 4**

OUR friend David was invited to give a talk to his local Rotary Group. Before proceedings began, the chairman reminded the gathering of the Four-Way Test followed by Rotarians around the world. Devised by Herbert Taylor in 1932, the Test says: "Of all the things we think, say or do, ask: Is it the truth? Is it fair to all concerned? Will it build goodwill and better friendships? Will it be beneficial to all concerned?"

David looked down at the sheets of paper in his hand and realised the chairman had just covered every aspect of his speech. And in far fewer words ...

But you'll be glad to hear he gave it anyway and it was well received.

Wednesday — **November 5**

IT was a line from an old country song on the radio that caught our friend Val's attention. Describing his sweetheart, the singer sang: "She could kiss the ground in winter time and make a flower grow."

It's a lovely image, even if you might get cold and your lips dirty trying it!

An impossible thing to do in real life, you would think. But not if the winter time concerned was in the heart of someone you knew, if the kiss was actually a word of encouragement and if the flower was the look of appreciation that blossomed in their eyes.

Thursday — **November 6**

I'D never heard this description of pessimism before. Describing an acquaintance the Lady of the House said, "Oh, she's always talking uphill."

Well, if it's possible to *always* have an "uphill" attitude, then it must be possible to spend as long talking "downhill", or chatting about the best in people and situations.

It seems to me the downward side of any hill is always the most fun!

Friday — **November 7**

JANET was on her way to see a friend. "She's going through a difficult time at the moment, so I'm going along to see if I can help," she confided to the Lady of the House. "I don't suppose I'll be able to do much, but at least I'll do what I can."

I suspect we've all been in Janet's position at some time. We want to be of assistance, but what can we achieve? Indeed, we sometimes feel so inadequate that we may stay away altogether. But who would not prefer to have a friend who comes to offer support?

Sometimes, just by showing that we care, we may achieve more than we ever realise.

WISE EYES

Saturday — **November 8**

IT'S rarely a comfortable feeling when our path through life suddenly twists and turns in a completely unexpected direction. Andrea Jaeger, as a world-famous young tennis player, seemed to be the perfect success story until an injury forced her out of the game at the age of only nineteen.

However, the behind-the-scenes story had not been so happy. Pressure from her tennis-coach father, plus the rivalry and loneliness of the tennis circuit had turned her into an isolated person, focused solely on the need to win.

But what Andrea did have was a deep faith, and when her career collapsed it was to God that she turned, never doubting that she would be guided. Using her newly-found free time, she decided to help sick children and set up a charity, Little Star Foundation, to assist those in need.

Then in 2006, she felt herself called to join the Dominican order of nuns and nowadays, fulfilled in her new life, is also happily reconciled with her family.

We may not always be able to choose the easiest route through life but I'm sure that if we can just trust, we will eventually find ourselves exactly where we are meant to be.

Sunday — **November 9**

THE best-selling Christian author Max Lucado describes himself as "the Minister of Writing and Preaching" at his church in San Antonio.

Who knew there was such a thing as a Minister of Writing? But doesn't it just go to show that God provided each of us with a talent, and when we use it well that can be our ministry? Now, who would like to be a Minister of Babysitting, Minister of Visiting Neighbours, or Minister of the Cheery Smile?

"He has made us competent as ministers of a new covenant – not of the letter but of the Spirit; for the letter kills, but the Spirit gives life." (Corinthians II 3:6)

Monday — **November 10**

DID you know that fossil records suggest there were roses in prehistoric times? We no doubt think of life then as being tough, basic, a real struggle for survival – but there were roses!

When we are going through difficult times in modern life, we should still look out for beauty. It will be there somewhere.

It always has been.

Tuesday — **November 11**

TREASURE YOURSELF

IT'S great to help others, to do what we may
To sort out their problems, to brighten their day,
To make time to listen, to show that we care,
To run a few errands; to simply be there.
Yet still there is someone – however life speeds –
Who's glad of your time, and who also has needs,
So just as important – be kind to them too,
And who is this someone? That someone is You!

Margaret Ingall

Wednesday — **November 12**

I SUSPECT that from time to time we've all been familiar with that sinking feeling of knowing that we've failed. We've fallen short of what we know we are capable of; we've let ourselves down, lost a chance that may never come again.

Well, if that happens to apply to you at present, take heart from these words from Oswald Sanders:

"Most Bible characters met with failure and survived … They came to know the God of the second chance, and sometimes the third and fourth."

In fact, I think God doesn't ever stop giving us chances. Just resolve next time to make the most of them.

Thursday — **November 13**

"MY grandmother used to say, 'If you can't say anything nice, don't say anything at all'." Andy smiled at the memory, then showed me these lines in a book he was reading:

Slander not, but speak kindness. If thou art provoked, speak not at once.

"These words were inscribed on a wall many centuries ago," he told me. "I have no idea who wrote them, but I bet it was somebody's grandmother!"

Friday — **November 14**

GREAT-AUNT Louisa, who was a children's author and illustrator in the early years of last century, kept a comprehensive and enduringly interesting diary throughout her life. She was also something of a deep thinker.

Her entry for November 14th stated: "Spent the afternoon at my church group in the hall where the Christian youth group had spent the morning. While there, I happened to catch sight of a brightly-coloured poster on the wall which proclaimed: *I cannot believe, because belief implies proof. I just know…* Now there is a young person who is sure of their way ahead."

Saturday — **November 15**

IMAGINE you could fulfil one of mankind's greatest needs! I'm sure the very thought of a task that huge would be enough to put a lot of people off.

Actually, all you need to do is smile, shake a stranger's hand in welcome or offer a listening ear. Philosopher and psychologist William James wrote: "The deepest craving of human nature is the need to be appreciated."

Appreciation might be the greatest, and simplest, gift you ever give.

Sunday — **November 16**

A GROUP of home décor experts on television one evening had gathered together some out-of-fashion furniture. They then decorated and restyled the items to make them just the thing for a modern flat.

They didn't call it recycling, they called it upcycling. They hadn't just re-used – in fact, they reckoned the originals now looked even better.

Faith does the same thing for us. You might think your life is fine before, but let God in and He will upcycle your world.

"Therefore, if anyone is in Christ, the new creation has come: The old has gone, the new is here!" (Corinthians II 5:17)

Monday — **November 17**

A N old proverb says: "Big doors turn on small hinges." Simple enough, but these small hinges must be well made from sound materials and be regularly maintained.

Our lives turn on small things like honesty, integrity, faith and trust. Let's attach ourselves to good "hinges" and make sure they, too, are well made, sound and regularly maintained.

Tuesday — **November 18**

D O you ever feel there's no way through your difficulties? John F. Kennedy came from a privileged background but he had his share of troubles, from a war wound that left him with lifelong pain to his many political battles. He had his victories as well, of course, so he knew what he was talking about when he said: "Every area of trouble gives out a ray of hope; and the one unchangeable certainty is that nothing is certain or unchangeable."

Find that ray of hope – and use it to change those dark days into brighter ones!

WINTER'S JEWELS

All IS WELL

"ALL is well,"
My Lord says,
As savage winds shriek
And maul the earth.
"All is well,"
He says to me,
As I tremble in the cold rain
That rises at my feet.
"All is well,"
He says,
As skies curdle
With the thick blackness of a storm.
I look into His eyes and whisper,
"All is well, my Lord,"
And a tender sprig of peace
Blossoms in my soul.
It grows.
It grows resilient in the wind,
Tall in the rain,
Resplendent in the storm,
And more beautiful
Each time it offers shelter
To those along the way.

Rachel Wallace-Oberle

Thursday — **November 20**

WHO can count the wonders of the world? And who can add to them? Well, I don't know anyone who can do the former, but I know each of us might do the latter.

A fellow by the name of Edwin Elliot, who must have been a keen observer of human nature, once wrote: "By being yourself, you put something wonderful in the world that was not there before."

Friday — **November 21**

WHEN you've stayed in a hotel you know that the scrap of soap you leave behind in the shower or wash hand basin will most likely be thrown away. Derreck Kayongo decided to do something about this wasteful practice.

His father was a soap maker in Uganda and when Derreck learned how much soap was thrown away by hoteliers in the United States, and that a total of two million children die each year worldwide due to a lack of sanitation, he established Global Soap Project.

Discarded hotel soaps are collected by volunteers across the United States and shipped to a warehouse in Atlanta. There the soaps are cleaned, reprocessed and packaged, then shipped and given at no cost to those who need them. More than 100,000 bars have been distributed to many communities in nine countries.

Derreck Kayongo says, "It's not good enough for us to complain about what other people aren't doing for us. It's important that we all band together, think of an idea and pursue it."

Saturday — **November 22**

I DON'T want to sound melodramatic," Lisa said, "but when my business failed, it felt as if my whole world had fallen apart. For a while it really shook my faith in every aspect of my life."

"But things did improve?" I asked.

She laughed. "They certainly did. It took some time, but I came to realise that life is still very much worth living. Things don't have to be expensive in order to be valuable, and just because someone doesn't have any money it doesn't mean that they're worthless."

It's wisdom well worth the learning. As Charles West once observed: "We turn to God for help when our foundations are shaking, only to learn it is God shaking them."

Sunday — **November 23**

A S WELL as being a wonderful tourist attraction, York Minster is a working church. Visiting it one day, our friend Barbara noticed there were several services being held in different chapels. Because of the acoustics and the size of the place the preachers make use of microphones and speakers, but they are kept low enough not to interfere with other services.

Wandering through the building, she walked into and out of the range of several sets of speakers. She heard one soft voice praising God, then it was replaced by another reading the Gospel, and so on.

In a fanciful moment she imagined she was hearing the voice of God wherever she went. Now, wouldn't that be a beautiful way to live a life; hearing God wherever we wandered and through whatever voice he chose to use?

"The Sovereign Lord has opened my ears; I have not been rebellious, I have not turned away."   (Isaiah 50:5)

Monday — **November 24**

H AVE you heard of the "As If" principle? William James, a philosopher and psychologist, came up with it at the end of the nineteeth century.

He suggested that people who weren't feeling cheerful, "sit up cheerfully, look around cheerfully, and act and speak as if cheerfulness was already there." Behaving like that, he insisted, would make you really cheerful in no time. The same principle was said to apply if you wanted to be braver, kinder, truer, more loving, more outgoing and so on.

Well, I know that if I smile when I don't feel like smiling, I soon feel like smiling. So I think there is something in this concept. Choose the way you want to live, and then act "as if" you already were those things.

And, you know, soon you will be!

Tuesday — **November 25**

TOM and Jane used all their savings to buy a small seaside hotel. Business was poor and after a few months they thought of selling up.

Then one morning, Tom opened a letter from a couple who had spent a weekend break with them. They thanked Tom and Jane for "a wonderful weekend" and said that they wanted to book for a longer stay. What's more, they were now recommending the hotel to all their friends.

"If it hadn't been for that letter," Tom told me, "we would have given up. What they said gave us the heart to carry on and within a few months we had found our feet and were very busy. That letter seemed to start off a whole new chapter for us."

Those few lines of thanks and encouragement were a turning point. This story is worth remembering if you know someone who's struggling against the odds.

Wednesday — **November 26**

IT was an interesting lesson in durability. The little book of uplifting stories which our old friend Mary bought in a jumble sale had been printed during the Second World War. It was probably read once or twice, then placed between two bigger books and forgotten, and then all these years later it had resurfaced and was eagerly purchased.

When Mary opened the pages, a little trickle of brown dust fell from the centre. The metal staples that had held it together, supposedly the toughest part, had rusted away. The cardboard front cover, the next strongest part, was tatty around the edges, while the pages, which probably hadn't been opened in decades, were fine. But the softest, most ethereal part of the book, the words of faith, joy and inspiration, were in pristine condition.

A story worth remembering the next time you wonder at the strength of soft words in an often hard world.

Thursday — **November 27**

I SUPPOSE it's only human nature to fear failure. No-one likes the thought of coming to grief, whether on a life-changing scale or merely looking a little foolish when a venture doesn't succeed.

Our friend John certainly wondered if he'd been foolish when he had to drop out of a sponsored long-distance trek because he simply couldn't keep up.

"But that failure certainly taught me a thing or two," he confided. "Like the importance of training properly. The trek will be held again next year, and I fully intend to finish it this time."

I'm glad John learned from his setback for, if we allow it, failure can often be our most helpful teacher. If you're still in doubt, consider these words by Carl F. Hughes:

"Falling into the deepest valley is nothing to fear. It just means that you are in the perfect position to climb the world's highest mountain."

Friday — **November 28**

H ERE are some quotes about the timeless quality of love to think about today:

"One can live magnificently in this world, if one knows how to work and how to love."   Leo Tolstoy

"Our job is to love others without stopping to inquire whether or not they are worthy. That is not our business and, in fact, it is nobody's business. What we are asked to do is to love, and this love itself will render both ourselves and our neighbours worthy."   Thomas Merton

"With love, we are creative. With it, we march tirelessly. With it, and with it alone, we are able to sacrifice for others."   Chief Dan George

"Love is that condition in which the happiness of another person is essential to your own."   Robert A. Heinlein

Saturday — **November 29**

THE Lady of the House came across this intriguing advertisement in a newspaper one day:

Clearance! All bad moods must go. So come on out and top up someone's parking meter, give up your seat on the bus or hold a door open. All it takes is a small gesture to brighten someone's mood. Help make the world a better place, one good deed at a time.

This had been placed by an organisation called People for Good. Readers were encouraged to join the movement and visit an Internet site that features suggestions and stories from people who have experienced the uplifting effects of a good deed.

The People for Good site states: "It may sound ambitious, but it's easier than you'd think. We're not asking for money, we just want you to donate a little generosity."

Surely a call worth answering, don't you agree?

Sunday — **November 30**

"WHEN my husband or sons are out late, I always leave lots of lights on for them," our friend Rose said. "I switch on the porch lights and the lamp in the living room window. There's nothing quite as welcoming as coming home to the warmth of light spilling through the windows into the darkness."

In the same way, our heavenly Father lights the path for us when we're uncertain of the way. With gentle words of encouragement, He takes our hand and illuminates each step, guiding us across treacherous, uneven ground that could cause us to stumble. And the closer we come to the end of our journey, the more clearly we see the safety and comfort waiting for us. There is no darkness that His light cannot dispel.

"For thou art my lamp, O Lord: and the Lord will lighten my darkness."   (Samuel II 22:29)

December

Monday — **December 1**

THE robin is one of the most popular British birds so it is no surprise that myths have grown up around it. It was said that it brought man the gift of fire, burning its breast in the process.

Another belief was that its breast was stained with Christ's blood when it tried to pull the thorns from His head. Glasgow's coat of arms contains a robin, a reminder that St Mungo brought one back to life through prayer.

Today there is no more welcome sight in the garden than the friendly robin redbreast.

Tuesday — **December 2**

DAVID and Julie were reminiscing about a relaxing holiday in York. "There was something really special about York, wasn't there?" said Julie.

"But let's not forget about Berwick," David reminded her. "There was a real sense of peace there."

"And what about the feeling of history in Winchester?" Julie asked.

"And even in bustling London we managed to find a relaxing place or two," David recalled. "Then there was Prague and Dublin, too."

"Do you think we just happened to find so many special places? Or did we take the 'special' with us?" Julie mused.

I can't speak for all of those places, but I do know that wherever David went he found Julie, and wherever Julie went she found David. If you take love with you, then any and every place becomes a special place.

172   The Friendship Book

BALANCING ACT

Wednesday — **December 3**

A N expert was explaining about Old Roses. These are the flowers that existed before selection and hybridisation gave us the modern roses which give us so much pleasure today.

Old Roses, he explained, don't bloom for as long as their modern counterparts and their petals have gentler shades. But they are hardy and don't require the same attention that modern varieties need, yet they still have the same scent their ancestors shared with the world.

I laughed and the expert wondered why. I explained that it had just occurred to me I knew several Old Roses. None of them were flowers, but all of them were beautiful.

Thursday — **December 4**

Y OU'VE decided you want to change. You want to behave differently, be the person you believe God wants you to be. But, well – it all sounds a bit daunting, so perhaps you'll leave it just for now.

If that's the way you're thinking, try reflecting on these words from an unknown author: "Do not ask the Lord to guide your footsteps if you are not willing to move your feet."

Just think about it – even if you only take one small step, you're already heading in the right direction.

Friday — **December 5**

I T can be so tempting. You happen to have heard a most fascinating snippet of gossip which you long to pass on. But that's the time to stop and remember the old proverb: "The words of the tongue should have three gate-keepers: Is it true? Is it kind? Is it necessary?"

Make sure your gate-keeper will only take "yes" for an answer!

Saturday — **December 6**

OVER the past few months Dorothy has faced a number of unexpected challenges. She confided to me one day that her faith was feeling a bit wobbly. Then she came across the dynamic words of Mother Teresa and her focus, she said, began to shift from worry and fear to gratitude. Dorothy said that she now approaches each day with an entirely new perspective having read these words:

"God made the world for the delight of human beings – if we could see His goodness everywhere, His concern for us, His awareness of our needs: the phone call we've waited for, the ride we are offered, the letter in the mail, just the little things He does for us throughout the day. As we remember and notice His love for us, we just begin to fall in love with Him because He is so busy with us. You just can't resist Him. I believe there's no such thing as luck in life, it's God's love, it's His."

Sunday — **December 7**

YOU can't visit Glasgow's Kelvingrove Art Gallery and Museum without spending some time in front of Salvador Dali's Christ of Saint John of the Cross.

It shows the crucified Christ high above some fishermen on the shores of the Lake of Galilee. If you look closely you will notice that there are no nails in Jesus' hands or feet. Dali himself said he thought they would spoil the image. But perhaps their omission was an unconscious reminder that this sacrifice was made willingly. In a sense the Lord hung himself there. For us.

Love is rarely about what is best for us, or what we can get from it. At its best it's always about what is willingly given.

"I beseech you therefore, brethren, by the mercies of God, that ye present your bodies a living sacrifice, holy, acceptable unto God, which is your reasonable service."

(Romans 12:1)

CHOSEN FOR YOU

Monday — **December 8**

HAVE you ever decided that something was just too difficult? Young Ben often did, and regularly abandoned projects at the first obstacle, until his father told him the story of the explorer Ernest Shackleton.

It was 1915 when, on an expedition to cross Antarctica via the South Pole, his ship "Endurance" became trapped in ice and, over a period of months, was totally crushed. Although they managed to survive by living on the floating ice, Shackleton knew they couldn't last much longer so, with five of his crew, went to get help.

This journey involved spending sixteen days crossing the ocean in a small boat, followed by a long and gruelling trek overland to reach a whaling station. It was an amazing enterprise, resulting in every man being saved.

"Difficulties are just things to overcome, after all," Ernest Shackleton was once quoted as saying.

Needless to say, young Ben's powers of perseverance have improved considerably!

Tuesday — **December 9**

THE concept of multi-tasking has been put to many good uses, but the most delightful one surely had to be when the Lady of the House asked our old friend Mary why she never seems to worry.

She assured me that she worries every bit as much as the rest of us, but she preferred to organise it. Rather than doing it in little chunks all through the day, she sets aside a whole hour each afternoon for her worrying.

"And because I like to multi-task," Mary continued with a straight face, "I schedule my afternoon nap for that same hour."

Well, no sense in worrying that she wouldn't have time for both, I suppose …

Wednesday — **December 10**

OUR friend Nicola moved to Pennsylvania a year ago and lives near an Amish community. Whenever she can she visits Amish craft fairs to see the wonderful artefacts made in traditional styles.

She explained that the Amish women, when they are making their big and beautiful quilts, like to include a patch that doesn't match the rest of the quilt. By their way of thinking it is a reminder that only God makes perfect creations.

It occurred to Nicola that the quilt would not be any the less cosy with that little non-matching patch. None of us are perfect but that doesn't mean we can't be useful. Like that quilt, we can still wrap ourselves around someone needing a little comfort, or do any number of other good things.

We might be like that little piece of patchwork, but just because we can't be perfect creations that doesn't mean we shouldn't still be beautiful ones.

Thursday — **December 11**

SOME think that large amounts of – well, anything, are the way to happiness. But author Iris Murdoch thought quite the opposite. She thought the secret of a happy life was "continuous small treats."

Small treats like putting your feet up, a visit to a friend, stroking a pet, tea with cake … Now, that sounds like a happy life to me!

Friday — **December 12**

OUR old friend Mary's clergyman always likes to put something meaningful on the outdoor church sign. Last Sunday she noticed he had posted this message: *The most important part of Christmas is the first six letters.*

So easy to forget in the hustle and bustle of the season, but so true!

Saturday — **December 13**

IT'S rather an old-fashioned expression now but someone who was dependable and decent, the kind of person you would like as a friend, used to be described as a "brick."

The term comes from ancient Sparta. A foreign emissary, visiting that often-embattled city state, asked where their defensive walls were. The king showed him the young men of their army and said each one of them was a brick in Sparta's walls.

I was reminded of that when I heard our friend Lynne describe friends as being like walls. Of course, I just had to ask what she meant.

"Oh, you know," she said. "Sometimes we lean on them and sometimes they are just comforting to have around you!"

The Spartans would have understood.

Sunday — **December 14**

IN 1952 the "Encyclopaedia Britannica" published its "Great Books Of The Western World." Mortimer Adler then published an introductory volume explaining the themes and characters contained in the books.

The "character" with the longest section devoted to them was God. When asked why, Adler explained: "More consequences for life follow from that one issue than any other." Rather than being too wordy, I suspect Mr Adler was prone to understatement!

"In the beginning God created the heavens and the earth."
(Genesis 1:1)

Monday — **December 15**

OF course, there is no such thing as the perfect life but even a difficult one can be a good one. As playwright Neil Simon said: "I love living. I have some problems with my life, but living is the best thing anyone has come up with so far!"

Tuesday — **December 16**

HERE is an ancient Sioux prayer to share with you today:

> Grandfather, Great Spirit all over the world,
> The faces of living things are alike.
> With tenderness, they have come up
>   out of the ground.
> Look upon your children that
>   they may face the winds
> And walk the good road
>   to the day of quiet.
> Grandfather, Great Spirit.
> Fill us with the Light,
> Give us the strength to understand
>   and the eyes to see.
> Teach us to walk the soft earth as relatives
>   to all that live.

Wednesday — **December 17**

THERE is nothing like music to herald the coming of Christmas. From the first hymns of Advent to the celebrations of midnight services, from the joyful sound that fills the shops to the simple tunes of children's carols, music weaves its magic.

Few people can be more associated with the sound of Christmas than musician John Rutter, whose compositions are among the best loved. This is why I was interested to see a television interview with him, in which he spoke of how the festive season allows us to make time for both ourselves and others:

"Christmas for me is a reminder of just how things might be – for just a few days each year. Normal life is put on hold. We have the world as it could be."

I love the thought of a world as it could be – and should be. Let us all do our best to make it so.

Thursday — **December 18**

A FRIEND sent Anna a video of a young man, who had found a wounded, orphaned baby bird on his lawn and nursed it back to health. He fed the tiny creature a mixture of sugar and water, and as it grew stronger, helped it to discover a feeder and flowering plants he'd placed in the room.

Perhaps the most touching moment was when the young man encouraged the bird to learn how to fly; he repeatedly moved his hand that the bird rested on, encouraging it to flutter to his other hand. Finally, he introduced the little creature to the outdoors.

Anna was amazed at the young man's compassion and patience and she realised that the images contained some of life's most beautiful principles. As William Wordsworth wrote: "That best portion of a good man's life; his little, nameless, unremembered acts of kindness and love."

Friday — **December 19**

WIDE, straight, easy roads. What more could a traveller want? Well, how about some delightful surprises? How about remembering that some things in life are more wonderful because of the obstacles we have to overcome to win them?

Environmentalist Edward Abbey put it like this: "May your trails be crooked, winding, dangerous – leading to the most amazing views. May your mountains rise into – and above – the clouds."

Saturday — **December 20**

DODIE SMITH, who wrote "101 Dalmatians", offered two cures for those days when we need something to raise our spirits: "Noble deeds and hot baths."

A fine reminder that there is a time for striving and a time for simply looking after yourself!

Sunday — **December 21**

DELLA was busy choosing between buying a fluffy rabbit or a teddy bear. "A friend's daughter has just had a baby," she explained. "I don't actually know her very well, but it's such an exciting event for them all that I want to be part of it."

There is something about the birth of a new baby that touches everyone. So how much more exciting is the birth of a baby whose arrival was to change everyone's lives:

"And she brought forth her firstborn son and wrapped him in swaddling clothes, and laid him in a manger because there was no room for them in the inn."   (Luke 2:7)

A baby born over two thousand years ago, a joy that will last forever!

Monday — **December 22**

IF you have read that classic work of comedy "Three Men In A Boat", then I'm sure you'll remember the moment when Jerome K. Jerome, suffering a minor ailment, picks up a medical dictionary to investigate further. Unfortunately, by the time he puts it down, he has managed to convince himself that there is almost no ailment from which he is not suffering.

It's hard not to smile at this particularly extreme display of pessimism, but in real life, it's not quite so amusing. No-one can be cheerful all the time, but to permanently look on the black side impairs every aspect of our life.

So let's try to make a resolution today to think and act as cheerfully as we can whenever possible.

Tuesday — **December 23**

IN a world that sometimes seems increasingly materialistic we may like to take a tip from Sir Wilfred Grenfell who served as a medical missionary in the early 1900s. He wrote: "The purpose of this world is not to have and to hold, but to give and to serve."

Wednesday — **December 24**

CHRISTMAS is my favourite time of year. It's a wondrous celebration of the ones we love and a joyful occasion to give generously and receive graciously. Here are some thoughts that eloquently express the beauty of this season:

"Christmas waves a magic wand over this world, and behold, everything is softer and more beautiful."

Norman Vincent Peale

"At Christmas, all roads lead home."　　Marjorie Holmes

"Blessed is the season which engages the whole world in a conspiracy of love!"　　Hamilton Wright Mabie

"Our hearts grow tender with childhood memories and love of kindred, and we are better throughout the year for having, in spirit, become a child again at Christmas-time."

Laura Ingalls Wilder

Thursday — **December 25**

FATHER, hear our prayer at Christmas,
Help us share the love You send,
Reaching out across the nations
Greet a stranger as a friend.
Thank You for the faith of Christmas
And the comfort we have found,
Knowing those who've gone before us
Once again will gather round.

As we share the cards and greetings,
Candles burning, clear and bright,
Help us reach the lost and lonely,
Bring them in to love and light.
Thank You for the hope of Christmas,
All our doubts and fears dispel,
In our hearts we know the meaning —
Love is endless, all is well.
　　　　　　Iris Hesselden.

Friday — **December 26**

THE hymn-writer John Mason Neale became well known after he wrote "Good King Wenceslas". It appeared in his "Carols For Christmastide" in 1853 and tells the story of the Bohemian king who is now patron saint of the Czech Republic and his care of the poor.

Although most think that John Neale came across the story during his travels in Europe, it is possible that he was inspired by a visit to the Pass of Killiecrankie in 1843. "On a sober Autumn day, in the jaws of the ravine, the grandeur is quite awful," he wrote. "At the bottom of the mountain there is a little glooming light, above there is a clear, cold north wind."

In an ancient gnarled tree he thought he recognised "an old grey-headed man, resting his head on his elbows". Perhaps, then, the lea of Beinn a' Bhreacaidh was the setting for the much-loved carol of the king and his page-boy who went to help a poor man collect wood "on the feast of Stephen".

Therefore Christian men, be sure,
Wealth or rank possessing,
Ye who now will bless the poor
Shall your selves find blessing.

Saturday — **December 27**

THE photograph in the glossy magazine showed a luxurious bedroom in a multi-million pound house. Beside the enormous bed was a cupboard, inside which was a water slide to the downstairs swimming pool.

It raised a good laugh before I started thinking of the things people look for in a house. When it came to what the Lady of the House and I look for, no water slides were involved. Instead we found ourselves agreeing with the librarian poet Sam Walter Foss who wrote: "Let me live in a house by the side of the road and be a friend to man."

It might not have a swimming pool, but I'm sure everything required would come to that house eventually.

FOLLOW ME

Sunday — **December 28**

CHROMATIUS, a 4th-century bishop of Aquileia, in today's north-eastern Italy, wrote that the road to heaven isn't long, and neither is it far away. But it does have rocks on it and it is up to us to move them.

What are those rocks? They are very real, earthly things like giving or taking offence, not loving justice, anything that separates people from each other. And, despite their apparent size, each of those rocks can be moved by the very weakest of us.

"As you go, proclaim this message: 'The kingdom of heaven has come near.' " (Matthew 10:7)

Monday — **December 29**

"OH, look!" the Lady of the House exclaimed one day as she looked through the newly-delivered mail. "We've been sent a postcard from Scotland – but the picture on the front is of an Italian chapel."

Our old friend Mary, who had sent the card, had also provided an explanation. The Chapel is on the tiny Orkney island of Lamb Holm, and was erected by some five hundred and fifty Italian prisoners of war who were sent there in 1942. With the men's morale low, the Commandant, Major T. P. Buckland, agreed to the Camp Padre's suggestion that they might build themselves a place to worship.

To one prisoner in particular, Domenico Chiocchetti, this was a God-given challenge. He had already built a statue of St George, made from barbed wire and concrete, but this was his chance to really put his talents to good use.

Soon all the men were working enthusiastically to construct a chapel which, by the time the war ended and the prisoners were due to depart, was so beautiful that the Lord Lieutenant of Orkney promised that it would always be looked after.

Today it still stands, an inspiring testament that even in times of terrible destruction, mankind can create beauty.

Tuesday — **December 30**

TODAY I'd like to share these anonymous words and I hope that you'll find them as inspiring as I do:

If the Earth were only a few feet in diameter, floating a few feet above a field somewhere, people would come from everywhere to marvel at it. People would walk around it, marvelling at its big pools of water, its little pools and the water flowing between the pools.

People would marvel at the very thin layer of gas surrounding it and the water suspended in the gas. The people would marvel at all the creatures walking around the surface of the ball, and at the creatures in the water.

The people would declare it as sacred because it was the only one, and they would protect it so that it would not be hurt. The ball would be the greatest wonder known, and people would come to pray to it, to be healed, to gain knowledge, to know beauty and to wonder how it could be.

People would love it, and defend it with their lives because they would somehow know that their lives, their own roundness, could be nothing without it. If the Earth were only a few feet in diameter.

"But as truly as I live, all the earth shall be filled with the glory of the Lord." (Numbers 14:21)

Wednesday — **December 31**

"TIME flies," said our old friend Mary, commenting on the passing of another year.

"It does," replied the Lady of the House, "but never any faster than one day at a time. And when you think of all the opportunities a single day brings to make things better, to lend a helping hand or to lift someone's spirits... Well, there ends up being more than enough time, if we use it wisely."

So, here's to 2015! Let's not look at it as a year that will fly by, but as a series of days of promise, each filled with opportunities to help.

PHOTOGRAPH LOCATIONS AND PHOTOGRAPHERS:

COLD SNAP – *The Wallace Monument and Ochil Hills from Stirling*
LOCHSIDE REFLECTIONS – *Loch Fyne*
CROCUS CARPET – *The Botanic Gardens, Glasgow*
IN THE GLOAMING – *Loch Ness from Dores Bay*
FOUNDED ON FAITH – *Inchcolm Abbey, Scotland*
AFTERNOON IDYLL – *Kinvara, Co. Galway*
BONNIE BANKS – *View from the Forest for a Thousand Years,
    Cashel, Loch Lomond*
BEAUTIFUL BORDERS – *Royal Victoria Park, Bath*
IN MEMORIAM – *St Peter's Church, Sark, Channel Islands*
BLUE HORIZON – *Applecross, Wester Ross*
PAISLEY PATTERN – *Paisley Abbey*
AWAY FROM IT ALL – *Whiteside Mountain, Cashiers, North Carolina, USA*
WHEN THE BOAT COMES IN – *Portuairk, Ardnamurchan*
SAFE STRONGHOLD – *Edinburgh Castle*
GOLDEN MOMENT – *Loch Tummel, Perthshire*
THE FALL – *New England, USA*
FOLLOW ME – *Borve Beach, Harris, Outer Hebrides*

ACKNOWLEDGEMENTS:

David Askham: In Memoriam. **Dennis Hardley**: Beautiful Borders. **T.G. Hopewell**: Paisley Pattern. **Lee Jackson**: Away From It All. **Douglas Laidlaw**: Lochside Reflections. **Jean-Louis Moray**: Nearly There! **Duncan McEwan**: Crocus Carpet, Blue Horizon, Follow Me. **Ian Neilson**: On the Rocks, Safe Landing. **Polly Pullar**: Best of Friends, Lean On Me, Wise Eyes, Winter's Jewels. **Phil Seale**: Cold Snap, Founded on Faith, Bonnie Banks. **Willie Shand**: A Hint of Spring. **Sheila Taylor**: When the Boat Comes In, Safe Stronghold, Golden Moment, The Fall. **thinkstockphotos.com**: Spring Smile, Balancing Act, Chosen For You. **Jack Watson**: In The Gloaming. **Richard Watson**: The Earth Awaits, Look! **Andy Williams Photo Library**: Afternoon Idyll.